LORING
'HAWAI'I

ıces of Power,
ʜistory, Mystery
& Magic

EXPLORING LOST HAWAI'I

Places of Power,
History, Mystery
& Magic

Crowe and Crowe

ISLAND HERITAGE™
PUBLISHING
A DIVISION OF THE MADDEN CORPORATION

ISLAND HERITAGE™
P U B L I S H I N G
A DIVISION OF THE MADDEN CORPORATION

94-411 Kō'aki Street
Waipahu, Hawai'i 96797-2806

Orders: (800) 468-2800
Information: (808) 564-8800
Fax: (808) 564-8877
islandheritage.com

ISBN 1-59700-590-8
First Edition, First Printing, 2008

Written by Ellie Crowe and William Crowe
Photography by William Crowe
Maps by Millennium Mapping L.T.D.
Sepia prints courtesy of Hawai'i State Archives
Edited by Rubellite Kawena Johnson
Book Design by Danvers Fletcher

CONTENTS

FOREWORD

The authors describe this book as a guide to sacred and historical sites that will increase cultural appreciation for Hawai'i by visitors and *kama'āina* alike. It is a cultural tour of places full of history, magic, mystery, and power to which Ellie Crowe brings her own unique background—she was educated in South Africa and spent twenty-five years in Australia, New Guinea, and New Britain— evoking both awe and respect for these sites. She and her husband, Will, have also sought explanations from local people who have special acquaintances with these places, adding the results of these interviews to their own observations. This provides a rich variety of experiences as we follow them on their journeys to Hawai'i's most sacred places.

Ellie Crowe writes with a fresh vitality and engaging style that recalls her appeal to a younger audience in her recent book *Little Princess Ka'iulani in Her Garden by the Sea* (Island Heritage, 1998). Her power of explication with evocation of wonder comes, perhaps, to some extent from her background in teaching. Her work also shows keen sensitivity to Hawaiian ways and feelings. This has an endearing quality, but the book is a serious guide for the tourist planning an interesting visit through the islands, whether the visitor intends to keep to the beaten track or explore the byways. Who knows? He may see the little *menehune* people himself, even in reverie, carrying stones from one valley to another, building temples in a single night while the whole world is fast asleep.

Rubellite Kawena Johnson

Hawai'i's historical sites can be found in our national parks, state parks, resorts, and visitor attractions. Many of the sites located in the national and state historical parks were identified in the 1960s as Hawai'i's most significant cultural resources and declared National Historic Landmarks. These landmarks include a large number of *heiau* sites that represent Hawaiian monumental architecture in their massive sizes, elaborate construction styles, and religious functions. A diversity of other Hawaiian site types were set aside for preservation, including fishponds, habitation complexes, adze quarries, and petroglyph fields.

A visit to one of Hawai'i's historical sites is an ideal way to discover Hawai'i's unique cultural heritage, but it is important to remember that these sites are fragile and irreplaceable. Many consist of stacked stone walls and stone paved floors—the foundations for *hale*, terraced fields of *kalo,* and complex ceremonial centers. Hawaiians did not use mortar, so these stone structures can easily collapse. When visiting the sites in this book, please respect and protect these fragile resources by practicing these guidelines:

- View the site from outside the structure. Stay on designated trails, and do not climb on or over rock walls. The stacked rock is unstable and may collapse.
- Rocks should not be moved, removed, or wrapped in *ti* leaves. This wrapping is not a traditional offering and may damage the site and the plants around it.
- Hawaiians traditionally left *ho'okupu* (offerings) such as fruit, vegetables, and fish. Offerings such as candles, incense, and coins can damage the sites and are not recommended.

There is a growing effort to heighten visitor awareness and understanding through interpretive signs, brochures, and books such as this one. We hope that visitors will realize that these sites are more than "just a pile of rocks"—these are places where people lived, farmed, fished, and worshiped. These are sites that remain sacred to the Hawaiian people, and they are reminders to all of us of Hawai'i's unique cultural heritage.

Martha Yent
Archaeology and Interpretive Programs
Division of State Parks, Department of Land
and Natural Resources, State of Hawai'i

There is a Hawai'i that most visitors never see. The Hawaiian Islands are full of beautiful white sand beaches and luxury resorts, but if you leave the sparkling coastline and venture into lonely valleys and onto windswept mountain paths, you might hear the beat of ancient drums or the whispers of ancestral voices. You might see the immense dark temples of powerful rulers and the remnants of ancient rocks where royal mothers gave birth to the fierce kings of long ago. Hawai'i is full of mysterious, hidden places where the remarkable events of the past are etched indelibly on the landscape and serve as a reminder of a rich cultural heritage.

In the last century many significant cultural and historical places have been damaged or destroyed by development. The western world has brought material values to Hawai'i and diminished the richness of traditional values. There is now a strong resurgence of Hawaiian pride and a raised cultural consciousness that is helping to regain some of the dying tradition. Tradition brings meaning to life and rekindles the sense of wonder that is one of the most precious parts of life. Exploring the traditions and stories of Hawai'i's past adds an enriching dimension to the lives of both *kama'āina* (children of the land) and visitors.

When you visit the historic and sacred places of the islands, imagine the people who lived on these sites hundreds of years ago. Imagine the *ali'i* (royalty) who stood on the high platforms of the *heiau* and surveyed the lands over which they ruled with absolute feudal power. Imagine an ancient kingdom.

The *ali'i* were very tall—both men and women reached heights of at least six feet (Kamehameha I was over seven feet in height). They wore cloaks as smooth as velvet made from thousands of brilliant red and yellow feathers, and their impressive feathered helmets had sweeping crests that resembled the comb of the fighting cock. Chiefesses wore coronets of feathers in their long, wavy hair, leis of mountain orchids, and necklaces made of ancestral hair and sea-ivory pendants. *Kapa* (tapa) cloths in soft hues were tied around their waists. The *kāhuna* (priests) wore white *kapa* cloaks draped over one shoulder and white *kapa* around their heads. Their ancient chants, strong and evocative, carry Hawaiian history and legend down to us through the ages.

Stand at a *heiau* on the night of a full moon and think of those who walked on these stones long, long ago; those who lived here in splendor or died in misery, who embraced a phallic rock and prayed for a child, or who thanked a fish god for a good day's catch. We are privileged to visit these places of energy and power.

The Ancient Hawaiians

The ancient Hawaiians had a poetic vision of the universe, in which the realm of the supernatural existed alongside the realities of daily life. People, plants, animals, and stones all possessed *mana* (spiritual power). Strict laws to protect and maintain the harmony of *mana* controlled all aspects of Hawaiian life.

To the Hawaiians *mana* was power, a force found in all substances. Possessing *mana* guaranteed vital strength and spiritual energy. With the possession of great *mana* came great knowledge, precognition, and control over matter. *Mana* came from the gods, and those closest to the gods had the most *mana*. The *ali'i* were born with it; they wore it like a cloak of power and traced their genealogies to the gods. To prevent *mana* from being diluted they married within the family. A king's marriage to his sister was not incest, it was a highly desirable union.

The *kāhuna* also possessed *mana* in abundance. Some used it to heal, some to destroy. They alone knew the formulas for health, prosperity, security, and victory in war. They prayed to the gods, who controlled life from birth to death, and they sacrificed food and animals. The gods consumed the "essence" of the offerings. For really important favors, the *kāhuna* sacrificed humans.

Hawaiians, praying for *mana,* knew and practiced deep forms of prayer. Some *heiau* are known to have been used for meditative prayer. During prayer ceremonies *'awa* (kava), an herbal drink that produces pseudo-mystical effects, was used. This helped people experience a mystic oneness with the gods of nature.

The *kapu* (sacred or forbidden) law protected the *mana* and helped maintain order in the world. Breaking a sacred or *kapu* law could have terrible consequences for the whole nation; the gods could become very angry and vengeful, causing volcanoes to erupt, tidal waves to form, or earthquakes to devastate the land. The *kapu* breaker had to be put to death.

The *kapu* put an aura of protective sanctity around a person or object. Chiefs were descendants of the gods, and their *mana* had to be protected. A very high chief might possess the *kapu moe*, and runners would go before him shouting out *"Kapu moe!"* as a warning. Everyone would immediately fall flat on the ground until the chief had passed. If the shadow of a commoner were to fall on the chief—or even his clothing, food, or water—that commoner would face an automatic sentence of death. Some merciful chiefs only left their houses in darkness to spare their subjects.

The system of *kapu* is Polynesian in origin and came to Hawai'i with the earlier Polynesian migration. It intensified in the thirteenth century with the introduction of the *luakini* (war and sacrificial) *heiau* and the war god, Kū, whose rituals demanded human sacrifice. The *kapu* system was very onerous for the common people, as all parts of their lives were governed by it. Men and women could not cook their food in the same oven or eat together. Women could not eat bananas or coconuts, and many types of fish were forbidden to women under punishment of death. But some *kapu* laws, such as the law governing the seasons of fishing, were beneficial in that they helped conserve fishing grounds.

The *heiau* is a sacred Hawaiian temple; a place of worship and sometimes sacrifice. The Hawaiian word *"hei"* means capture or summon, and *"au"* implies an invisible current of energy or power. The *kāhuna* chose the correct place to build a *heiau* after consulting with the gods. Scholars have investigated the probability of the alignment of some *heiau* to celestial objects. They theorize that ancient Hawaiians were probably familiar with mathematical alignments called leylines and possibly with a global grid composed by these lines. The most powerful *heiau* were placed to align with each other and the celestial phenomena.

Archaeologist Tom Lethbridge developed the theory that a leyline is an energy line joining places with high concentrations of the earth's force field. Places that were sacred to old pagan religions are frequently found on leylines, including ancient sites of Britain (some with cathedrals erected over them), the Nazca lines across the Peruvian desert, roads across the desert surrounding Chaco Canyon, Irish faery paths, Chinese *lung mei* (spirit lines), German *geisterwege* (ghost paths), and the death roads or *doodwegen* of the Netherlands. The lines usually link places of power (Heselton 1999, 16, 17, 18, 58–67). Some *luakini heiau* are thought to follow a leyline that joins the sacrificial *heiau* of Tahiti, Samoa, and the Marquesas.

The size of a *heiau* and the amount of labor involved in building it is an indication of the power of the *ali'i* and the *kāhuna*. The rocks were carefully chosen, and they were brought from afar by lines of people who passed them hand-to-hand. *Heiau* were built for many purposes, including healing, fishing, agriculture, and war. Most *heiau* were built on rectangular rock platforms. Some had terraces and steep walls, others had walled enclosures.

When you visit a *heiau*, imagine how it looked five hundred years ago. The *luakini heiau* had twenty-foot-high oracle towers for communication with the gods. The towers were built of wood and covered with *kapa*. Ferocious *ki'i* (wooden images) of the gods, with pearl-shell eyes staring and dog teeth glistening, guarded the *heiau* and watched over the altar. Thatched structures housed the sacred drums and sacred water. There was a pit for the bones.

The Hawaiians stressed the importance of *mālama 'āina*—serving and caring for the land. Remember that these are ancient and fragile sites of great cultural significance to the Hawaiian people many of whom regard the sacred monuments as filled with *mana*. Prayer ceremonies and offerings continue there today.

ACKNOWLEDGMENTS

After living in Hawai‘i for twelve years, we are still lost in the beauty of the islands and fascinated by their history. We loved reading about the great Kamehameha, the gentle Keōpūolani, the beautiful, proud Ka‘ahumanu, the tattooed, mighty Kahekili, and the powerful, shrewd *kāhuna*. We apologize for any errors and feel fortunate not to have to prostrate ourselves in the mud, face down, before the *ali‘i,* or to experience a fate much worse!

Writing this book has been an enriching and very enjoyable experience, and many people have contributed to it. Thank you to Dale Madden, president of Island Heritage, for making it all happen; to Professor Rubellite Kawena Johnson for patient editing, and for being so gracious always; to Sarah Wageman for careful editing and assistance; to Martha Yent, Department of Lands and Natural Resources, State Parks Division, for giving valuable time and information; and to the archaeologists at the State Historic Preservation Division. Thanks also to Dr. Sinoto and the staff of the Bishop Museum, the helpful librarians at Hawai‘i Kai and Aina Haina Public Libraries, the State of Hawai‘i Library, and the State Archives.

Thank you to Juliet Fry and Caroline Bennet, our lovely daughters, for inspired and enlivening contributions; to Adam Crowe, our son, and Eric Bennet, for help with the computer, and to Aaron Fry for information on art and sculpture in the Pacific. Thank you, Barbara Ka Mille, Marc Schechter, and Charles Fujimoto for advice on photography.

Mahalo to the people who so generously shared their culture and stories with us: Buddy Peters, Jacob Mau, Daniel Kikawa, Mickey Ioane, Mama Loa, the Morgan family—Margo, John, and Francis, Fern Kalehuamakanoe Pule, Linda Beech, Mareko Richmond, Anna Goodhue, Miriam Baker, Ronald Kikumoto, Kapono Hamilton, Matthew Hammond, Tava Taupu, Lona Moniz, Willy the *ti* leaf weaver, Francine Dudoit, San Tomacder, Ken Dudoit,

Chris and Lew Trusty, and Lyndon de la Cruz. We are grateful to Chipper Wichman, Director of Kahanu Garden, for taking us to the top of Piʻilanihale Heiau and to his lovely and patient wife, Hauoli; to Professor David Saunders for permitting us to visit the University of Hawaiʻi Observatory on the top of Mauna Kea; to the staff of the Hawaiʻi Ghost Tour; to Eddie Pu, Mike Townsend, and to all the informative and friendly park rangers at the National Park Service; to Ric Elhard of Kula Kai Caverns and Chuck Thorne of Maui Cave Adventures for taking us underground; to Jack Spruance, manager of Puʻu o Hoku Ranch for allowing us to visit the Sacred Grove of Lanikāula; to Kalama, Hawaiian kupuna, and members of Wahiawā Civic Club; and to Gigi Valley, Public Relations Manager, Sol Kahoohalahala, Cultural Director and kupuna, and Bonnie Phelps, Public Relations Coordinator, Lānaʻi Company, for sharing their treasured island of Lānaʻi.

Thank you to the friendly staff of Alamo Rent-A-Car for the miles of smiles.

Mahalo to the friends who listened, gave suggestions, interviewed people, hiked through torrential rain, rode mules, braved gale force winds on Mauna Kea, tested mai tais at Tahiti Nui, watched molten lava, breathed sulfur fumes, and traversed graveyards: Jim and Sandy Rodin, Liz Womersley, Annette White, Caroline Hoff, Phil and Fé Bennet, Chris Womersley, Ray Coates, and Margaret and Sally Teh. *Mahalo* for helpful advice from critique group writers: Christopher Kingsley Sur, Shan Correa, Nancy Pinkosh, Lauren Bjorkman, Bob Tyson, Elaine Masters, Jean Gochros, and Lynne Wikoff.

This book is dedicated to Phyllis Coates, writer and historian, for your constant enthusiasm and inspiration—thank you, Mommy!

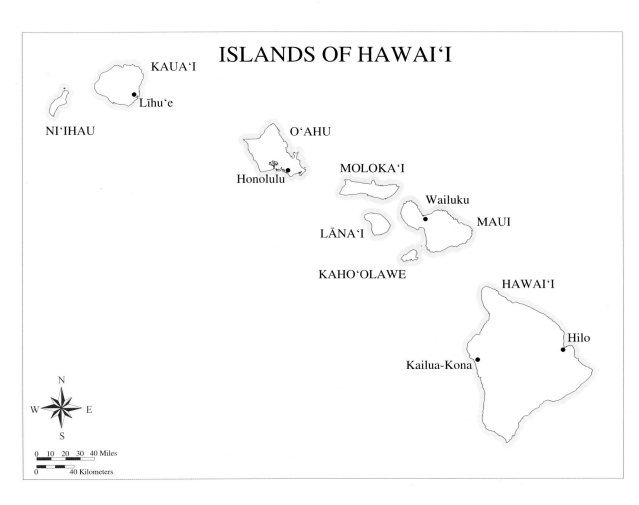

ISLANDS OF HAWAI'I

KAUA'I

Līhu'e

NI'IHAU

O'AHU

Honolulu

MOLOKA'I

Wailuku

LĀNA'I

MAUI

KAHO'OLAWE

HAWAI'I

Hilo

Kailua-Kona

N
W   E
S

0 10 20 30 40 Miles
0   40 Kilometers

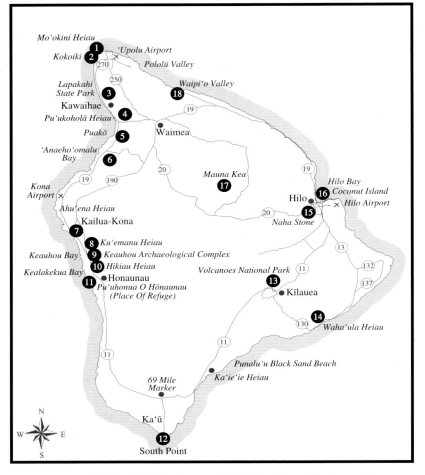

1. Mo'okini Heiau, Kohala District-
Immense sacrificial temple

Fear falls upon me on the mountain top

Fear of the passing night

Fear of the night approaching

Fear of the pregnant night

Fear of the breach of the law

Dread of the place of offering and the narrow trail

Dread of the food and the waste part remaining

Dread of the receding night

Awe of the night approaching.

-from "Kumulipo," the Hawaiian creation chant
(Beckwith 1972, 92)

Massive Mo'okini Heiau showing path to altar, and entrance on left.

Mo'okini Heiau looms over the wide, windswept northern plains of the island of Hawai'i. A huge (280 feet long by 140 feet wide) and impressively preserved *heiau*, its dark walls of carefully laid stones rise 19 feet high. Tradition says that the stones for the ancient *heiau* came from Pololū Valley, eight miles distant, and were passed hand-to-hand by a chain of eighteen thousand men. Imagine the power of the warrior chiefs who commanded the building of this immense temple.

Some historians believe that during the thirteenth century, warlike Tahitians arrived in the Hawaiian islands, possibly drawn to these volcanic islands because the forces of nature were so apparent here and the *mana* was so strong. One of the new arrivals on the island of Hawai'i was a powerful Tahitian *kahuna*, Pā'ao. He thought the Hawaiian chiefs did not command enough respect and that their gods were too weak—an intolerable condition. He sent for a powerful high chief from Tahiti, Pili, who did much to restore the respect due to high chiefs on the island of Hawai'i. Pā'ao also intensified the *kapu* system, brought in a new design for *heiau*, and introduced the hungry war god, Kū, whose rituals demanded human sacrifice.

Mo'okini Heiau, originally a smaller temple built as early as A.D. 480, was enlarged following Pā'ao's arrival. The *heiau* became part of a terrible chain of *luakini heiau* extending across Polynesia. Pā'ao brought

Island of Hawai'i

the altar stones from his home temple Taputapuatea (Sacrifices from Abroad), the largest and most feared temple in Polynesia. Boulders from this temple were transported hundreds of miles across the sea to serve at new temples. Such a boulder, with a human victim buried beneath it, gave a new temple great prestige.

A large phallic rock stands at the northern wall of the *heiau*. Next to this is an ominous-looking large slab of lava rock, with a shallow hollow at the top. This was the *holehole* stone, where the baked bodies of sacrificed victims were laid and the flesh was stripped from their bones.

Phallic rock and holehole stone outside walls of heiau.

These valuable bones were used for fish hooks and other implements. Countless numbers of Hawaiians were sacrificed at this war *heiau.*

Among the ruins is the foundation of a building for the *Mū*, the body catcher. This person was responsible for obtaining victims for the *heiau*, and the cautious would hide at his approach. Parents would threaten naughty children, "Behave or the *Mū* will get you!"

(References: Joesting 1972, 15; Kikawa 1994, 140, 142; Kirch 1985, 259; Kirch 1996, 118; Malo 1996, 99; Stokes 1991, 173-78.)

We stopped the rental car at the small airport parking area and looked with dismay at the muddy road, filled with potholes, that led to the heiau. We decided to walk and set off bravely under the boiling midday sun. Fortunately, the aloha spirit soon stepped in to help us out-a young family with a four-wheel drive jeep stopped and gave us a ride.

1. Moʻokini Heiau

We wandered around the huge outer walls and peered into the gloomy interior of the *heiau*. I didn't want to venture inside-it had an ominous atmosphere. I pictured *kāhuna* performing rituals before hushed audiences who would squat motionless for hours in frightened reverence, since one wrong movement during such ceremonies resulted in death.

A large phallic rock stood near the entrance to the site. We stopped to photograph it and noticed a raised altar slab nearby with an offering on it. At first glance, the offering appeared to be a protea. Pale pink sections, fluted with beige stripes, fluttered in the breeze.

"Do you see the owl?" the driver of the jeep asked.

We reluctantly went closer and looked in horror. The offering was a beautiful bird, an owl, lying dead, with its wings spread out on the altar. A large round rock held down its head.

"I can't believe this," the driver said. "The owl is the 'aumakua (family god) of the family of *kāhuna* responsible for this *heiau*. Why would anyone want to kill one? There must be some kind of *kāhuna* warfare going on here."

The following day we met Pastor Daniel Kikawa, author of the book Perpetuated in Righteousness. We told him about the sacrificed owl.

"That's very strange," he said. "The owl is regarded by many Hawaiians as a sacred bird. I think it would be considered very unlucky to kill one. Sometimes strange cults use the *heiau*, and they have their own interpretations of rituals."

He told us that according to his research, Mo'okini Heiau was originally built by priests of 'Io, the one true creator god of the Hawaiian people. He introduced us to Mickey Ioane, a strong, gentle Hawaiian man who "talked story" with us.

The *heiau* is on Mickey's family land, and when he was a boy his grandfather often told him, "You are the Chosen One."

Mickey didn't understand what he meant but thought he might receive a nice inheritance some day. For years Mickey felt a tug to go back to Kohala but didn't know why. A series of episodes led him to ask his aunt, Josephine Moke, a genealogist and historian, why he felt the need to go to Mo'okini Heiau. She asked him what he felt he needed to achieve, and he answered that he needed "To make things right."

She then told him that his ancestors had been high priests of 'Io who were killed or forced to flee by priests of Pā'ao, who dedicated the temple to the war god, Kū. His ancestors kept 'Io in their hearts and for generations chants to 'Io were kept secret. She felt that Mickey had been chosen to take the *heiau* back for 'Io.

Island of Hawai'i

Mickey still resisted this responsibility, but he ended up feeling like Jonah, resisting God's word. Finally, in March 1998, Mickey and others prayed over Mo'okini Heiau, rededicating it to 'Io and asking 'Io's forgiveness for the human sacrifices perpetrated there. As Mickey stood praying at the altar, he noticed that people in front of him were pointing over his shoulder. He turned around and saw a whale leaping out of the ocean and a perfect rainbow arching across the sky.

Mickey composed the beautiful song "Hawai'i 78" when he was a tenth grade student. The words have new meaning for him now:

Cry for the gods and cry for the people
Cry for the land that was taken away
And then yet you'll find Hawai'i.

(Mickey Ioane, "Hawai'i 78," sung by Israel Kamakawiwo'ole.)

Directions: From Kawaihae, travel to the 20-mile marker, turn left at the sign for 'Upolu Airport, and proceed two miles. When you reach the airport, you will see a potholed dirt road marked with a sign, which leads 1.6 miles to the *heiau*.

The birth site of Kamehameha I is 0.4 miles past the *heiau*. (See Site 2-Kokoiki)

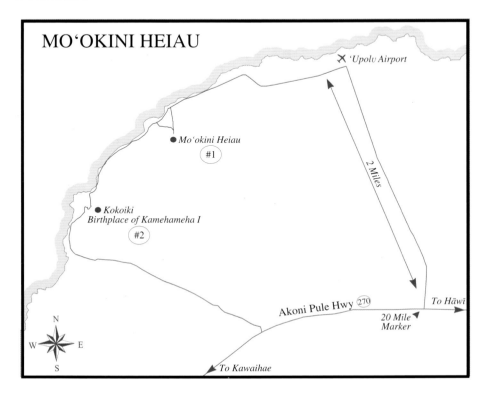

MO'OKINI HEIAU

'Upolu Airport

Mo'okini Heiau
#1

Kokoiki
Birthplace of Kamehameha I
#2

2 Miles

Akoni Pule Hwy 270

To Hāwī

20 Mile Marker

To Kawaihae

N W E S

1. Mo'okini Heiau

2. Kokoiki, Kohala District–
Birthplace of Kamehameha I

> *Like the heavy rains of 'Ikuwā is the chief,*
> *Intense is the heat in the vast heavens*
> *To Makali'i belong the intensely warm days,*
> *In which was born the chief, a fighter.*
> -Hawaiian chant (Kamakau 1992, 68)

THIS ISOLATED place was the scene of high drama in the middle of the eighteenth century. As thunder boomed and Halley's comet streaked across the sky, a child was born at this windswept place.

For years *kāhuna* had prophesied the birth of a child who would grow up to be a mighty warrior and conquer and rule all the islands. This prophecy greatly disturbed Alapa'inui, the ruling chief of the island of Hawai'i. He became even more concerned when his niece, the pregnant high chiefess Keku'iapoiwa, made public her desire to eat the eyeball of a shark. Alapa'inui regarded this as a fearful omen, especially since he was already suspicious about the parenthood of the

Island of Hawai'i

coming baby. Keku'iapoiwa had left her husband on Hawai'i to spend months visiting her *ali'i* family on Maui, and she returned pregnant. The Maui chief, the mighty, tattooed Kahekili, was Alapa'inui's sworn enemy. Was he also the father of Keku'iapoiwa's unborn child?

Frightened by rumors and threats, Keku'iapoiwa fled to the isolated plains of Kohala. The child born in this lonely place was immediately handed to a trusted warrior, Nae'ole, who ran the long distance to Waipi'o Valley with the newborn infant. Nae'ole gave the baby to his wife, who was nursing her own baby daughter.

When the news of the birth of a male child reached the court, Alapa'inui raged. He ordered his warriors to kill the baby. On Maui, Kahekili's family, who did not want any potential rivals, gave similar orders.

Warriors came to the cave, but Nae'ole's wife told them her little daughter was the only baby there. Little Kamehameha lay snugly hidden under *kapa* cloths, and the warriors returned to Alapa'inui empty-handed.

The birth site consists of a large stone-wall enclosure with an entrance on the side away from the sea. All that remains inside are large boulders that are believed to be the same birthing stones on which Keku'iapoiwa gave birth to the infant destined to become Kamehameha the Great, the future mighty warrior and ruler of the islands.

(Reference: Kamakau 1992, 67-68.)

Directions: From Mo'okini Heiau, continue along the dirt trail for 0.4 miles.

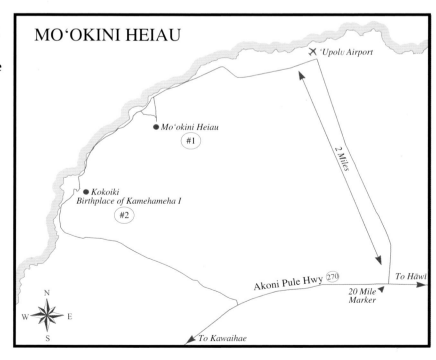

MO'OKINI HEIAU

'Upolu Airport

Mo'okini Heiau
#1

Kokoiki
Birthplace of Kamehameha I
#2

2 Miles

Akoni Pule Hwy 270
20 Mile Marker
To Hāwī

To Kawaihae

N
W — E
S

Historic house - probably abandoned only a few decades ago. Inset images clockwise from upper left: Fish shrine for offerings to fish god, Kū'ula, a fisherman's tool - a fishnet, and a kōnane (checkers) board

3. Lapakahi State Park, Kohala District-
Ancient fishing village

What a mistake my daughter has made
In marrying a husband who hews out canoes.
He hews out the canoe and leaves it in the forest.
He returns and takes the pig of the innocent and bakes it.
What a mistake to have a hewer of canoes as a husband.
-Hawaiian chant (Fornander 1959, 58)

KOAI'E, A six-hundred-year-old fishing village that was once known as a gathering place for practitioners, teachers, and students of healing, has been partially restored, and it provides unique insight into life in ancient Hawai'i. Hot, dry trails wind past platforms and terraces, canoe sheds, and fishing shrines. Stone boards for *kōnane* (Hawaiian checkers) and round stones for bowling wait for players of long ago to return. Cool breezes blow from across the sparkling water, and rainbow fish dart at the edge of the rocky shore. Interpretive signs assist visitors in understanding the daily life of the ancient Hawaiian people.
(References: Interpretive pamphlet, National Parks Service; Kirch 1985, 177-78.)

Island of Hawai'i

In November 1998 dozens of practitioners and students of lomilomi and lāʻau lapaʻau gathered at Lapakahi State Historical Park for a conference called "Pathway Returning to Heaven." Under a waning full moon, they rededicated the sacred site as a place where traditional healing practices could be learned and knowledge could be passed on from generation to generation.

Governor Cayetano signed a law in July 1998 enabling Native Hawaiian healers to become licensed practitioners. There are more than two hundred practitioners of the arts of Hawaiian healing in the islands who have learned their skills from relatives or *kāhuna*. Many elderly Hawaiian healers say they are passing down their knowledge to their children. Some are worried, however, because the *kāhuna* are growing old, and development and pesticides are causing herbs to die.

Other healers warn that insufficient knowledge of herbs is a dangerous thing. Taking excess amounts of *ʻawa*, a drink gaining popularity because of its relaxing effects, can cause skin to peel. *Kukui*, a standard Hawaiian cure-all, can cause diarrhea if taken in large amounts.

Auntie Margaret Machado, an eighty-two-year-old practitioner from the island of Hawaiʻi, has students from Europe and Australia. She draws her inspiration from religion and intuition. Christianity played a major role in the healing methods of Papa Kalua Kaiahua. He had his patients open the Bible and used the scripture on the page they selected to treat their problem. He also used herbal ointments and massage. He said that if patients hurt, he would take care of them.

(Reference: Answar 1998.)

Directions:
From Kawaihae, take Highway 270 north for twelve miles. Turn *makai* (toward the sea) to the parking lot of the state park. Hours: 8 a.m. to 4 p.m. daily.

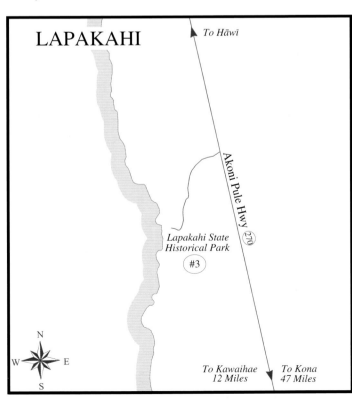

4. Pu'ukoholā Heiau, Kohala District-
War temple to Kū

> *Fallen is the Chief, overthrown in the kingdom,*
> *Gasping in death, scattered in flight;*
> *An overthrow throughout the land;*
> *A hard panting from the rapid flight;*
> *Countless the numbers from the universal route,*
> *The night declares the slaughter.*
> *There extended lay my conquering night,*
> *Mine own night, dark and blinded,*
> *Falling on the road, falling on the sand;*
> *The sovereignty and the land*
> *United in Chief, are passed away.*
> -from the "Haui ka Lani," this canto is a prophecy of the
> death of Keōua, who was sacrificed by Kamehameha I at this *heiau*
> (Handy et al. 1965, 183)

Island of Hawai'i

"HONOR THE supreme war god, Kūkā'ilimoku. Build a huge *luakini heiau* at Pu'ukoholā," the prophet Kapoūkahi told Kamehameha I. "If you do this, you will gain the whole kingdom without a scratch to your skin."

Kamehameha I built the massive stone temple on a hill four hundred feet above the sea overlooking Kawaihae harbor. This sacred structure, measuring 100 by 224 feet, with immense 20-foot-high lava walls and terraces, was constructed between 1790-91. Workers formed a human chain twenty miles long to transport rocks hand-to-hand from the seaside village of Pololū to Pu'ukoholā. Thousands of workers labored, and even Kamehameha himself helped with the building. *Kāhuna* were everywhere, attending to rituals vital to the temple's success.

Because this was a *luakini heiau* consecrated to the war god, Kū, a human sacrifice was required. The sacrifice it received was a very prestigious one-Kamehameha's cousin. When Kamehameha invited Keōua, his cousin and chief rival, to the dedication ceremony, Keōua received the invitation with suspicion. He was responsible for the earlier killing of the women and children of Hāmākua, and he feared Kamehameha's revenge. Ignoring the invitation, however, could cause Kamehameha to invade Keōua's home territory of Ka'ū.

Keōua had been having bad luck. It appeared he could no longer count on the blessing of the goddess Pele, who had rained hot ashes down on his warriors, killing over four hundred men, women, and children, leaving prints of their dying footsteps embedded in the lava fields of Ka'ū. He set off reluctantly to the dedication ceremony. According to tradition he cut off the tip of his penis en route, thereby indicating that he would have no offspring.

When Keōua's canoe landed at the beach fronting Pu'ukoholā *Heiau*, a skirmish broke out. Keōua was killed by a spear thrown by the warrior Ke'eaumoku, and almost all of his companions were slain. Keōua's body was taken to the *heiau* and offered as the principal sacrifice to Kū. The prophecies came true, and by 1810 Kamehameha I was the king of all the Hawaiian islands.

In August 1991 descendants of Hawaiians who took part in Keōua's death came to Pu'ukoholā to offer prayers, chants, and offerings. Wearing authentic feathered capes and helmets and carrying tall feathered *kāhili*, descendants from both rulers' families, some from as far away as New Zealand, embraced and tried to heal the deep hurt still engraved in their hearts. Some descendants of Kamehameha, however, say that this ceremony was intended to make Kamehameha look bad,

4. Pu'ukoholā Heiau

Altar of the heiau with massive walls behind

and that he was nowhere nearby when Keōua was killed.

Mailekini Heiau is just downhill. This temple, originally crowded with idols, was later converted into a fort by Kamehameha I, and twenty-one cannons defended Kawaihae against the chiefs of Maui, Lānaʻi, Molokaʻi, Kauaʻi, and Oʻahu. The man responsible for the military conversion was John Young, a captured British sailor who became Kamehameha's trusted adviser and friend.

Under the deceptively peaceful blue water of Kawaihae Bay, offshore from Puʻukoholā Heiau, are the remains of a shark *heiau*, Hale-o-Kapuni, where human remains of the *heiau*'s victims were

Island of Hawaiʻi

Expansive view of Kawaihae Harbor from the heiau

offered to sharks. There is a leaning post at the shore where the chief stood as he watched the circling sharks consume the offerings. (References: Emory 1965, 83; Handy et al. 1965, 183; Kamakau 1992, 150, 154-57; Kirch 1985, 175; Interpretive pamphlet, National Parks Service.)

We stood in the hot sun at the foot of the huge heiau and watched with fascination as a man and woman performed what seemed to be a blessing or a dedication ceremony. The man had his hand on the woman's head and both prayed earnestly.

"To whom are they praying?" I asked my part-Hawaiian companion. "Do they pray to the old Hawaiian gods?"

"Maybe," she replied. "People say that there are shark gods in the ocean here. They come because of all the sacrifices." She pointed to the ocean. "Blood still seeps from the rocks into the water of the bay."

4. Pu'ukoholā *Heiau*

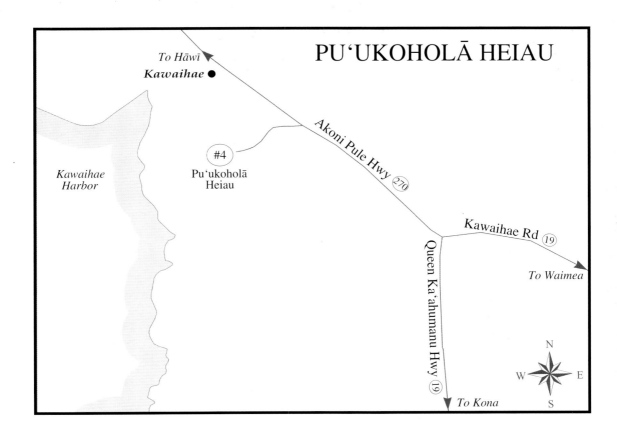

PUʻUKOHOLĀ HEIAU

To Hāwī
Kawaihae ●

Kawaihae Harbor

(#4)
Puʻukoholā
Heiau

Akoni Pule Hwy (270)

Queen Kaʻahumanu Hwy (19)

Kawaihae Rd (19)

To Waimea

To Kona

N
W E
S

Directions: From Kawaihae, drive south on Highway 270 for one mile. Instructions for a self-guided tour and a color brochure are available at the visitor center. Hours: 7:30 a.m. to 4 p.m. daily. Picnics and swimming are possible at nearby Spencer Beach Park.

Island of Hawaiʻi

5. Puakō Petroglyphs, Kohala District-
Picture albums from the past

THIS FAMOUS petroglyph field has over three thousand glyph units that were carved between 1000 and 1800 A.D. The petroglyphs are along a portion of the ancient Mālama Trail that runs past the beautiful Mauna Lani Bay Hotel and Bungalows. You can easily access the petroglyph fields from Holoholokai Beach Park at the northern end of Kanikū Drive.

The petroglyphs were drawn in a *pāhoehoe* lava flow. This type of lava flows rapidly, forming low mounds with smooth surfaces. Petroglyphs on this type of glazed surface show up very well, and the sight of all these drawings on squares of lava is quite amazing. Who were the people who crossed the fields of spiky lava and spent hours in the hot sun laboriously scraping these images? Were these accounts of notable events, prayers to the gods, or doodles made to pass the time?

Walking down the shady ancient trail, you will see carved human or anthropomorphic figures, animals, and geometric figures. Most of the petroglyphs are just past a dirt road intersection, which is about a fifteen minute walk. Look for the running men, the fighting paddle men, and the long line of twenty-nine stick figures marching in single file. A touching scene depicts the birth of an *ali'i* infant. The father is holding the baby's feet, and the child has rays coming out of his head to denote his importance. Are these lava fields of South Kohala sacred sites? Petroglyphs are often associated with sacred ceremonial and *kapu* sites, and historians assume that they have some magic or religious function. Supernatural figures were often symbolized by animals-dog motifs may refer to Kaupē, the ghost dog, whose presence often warned of danger; and *mo'o*, which are lizard-like figures, may be representations of *'aumākua* or *'unihipili*, protective spirits in animal form.

There are also a number of small holes and circles, which held the navel cords of babies. Often the *'aumakua* is portrayed beside the *piko* (navel) hole.

Along nearby Puakō Road is Hōkūloa Church, built by Reverend Lorenzo Lyons in 1859. This much-loved missionary, who spent fifty-five years in the islands, composed Hawai'i's unofficial anthem, the ballad "Hawai'i Aloha." He played a major role in leading 96 percent of the Hawaiian population to Christianity by 1853.

Kalāhuipua'a Fishpond on the grounds of the Mauna Lani Resort

The ancient Kalāhuipua'a Trail, a ribbon of dark lava, meanders through the lush grounds of the Mauna Lani Resort. There was once an underground city here, in a complex of lava caves used by ancient Hawaiians. The clear, green Kalāhuipua'a Fishponds were sacred to the *ali'i* who enjoyed their fresh fish and rich varieties of marine life. Kamehameha the Great maintained a fishing village here, and a replica of his canoe marks his landing site.

(References: Cox and Stasack 1970, 85; McBride 1969; Schmitt 1977.)

Sunset is a perfect time to walk this trail and view the petroglyphs, but don't stay too late—night marchers also use this ancient trail!

One of the most convincing, and consequently most blood-chilling, stories of the sighting of these processions of dead chiefs and warriors was told by Reverend Lorenzo Lyons, who saw a great company of chiefs, warriors, and food bearers walking in procession in South Kohala.

"They were people of the spirit," he explained. "God has given both material and spiritual forms."

This area of South Kohala is steeped in history, and on the night of the full moon Kaniela Akaka, the Hawaiian historian at the Mauna Lani Bay Hotel, holds a twilight gathering. Everyone is invited: resort guests, members of the public, and those of the next world, to sit under the stars and listen to stories and music and experience ho'okipa (Hawaiian-style hospitality). Call (808) 367-2323 for more information.

Directions: From Kailua-Kona, follow Highway 19 about twenty-four miles north. Turn left onto Mauna Lani Drive and at the roundabout turn right on North Kanikū Drive. Proceed to Holoholokai Beach Park and follow the signs to the petroglyphs. A small turnout and a wooden sign indicate a walking trail. The best petroglyphs are at the end of a pleasant, shady fifteen-minute walk.

The Kalāhuipua'a Fishponds and trail are on the grounds of the beautiful Mauna Lani Bay Hotel. There is a comprehensive pamphlet available at the hotel's front desk.

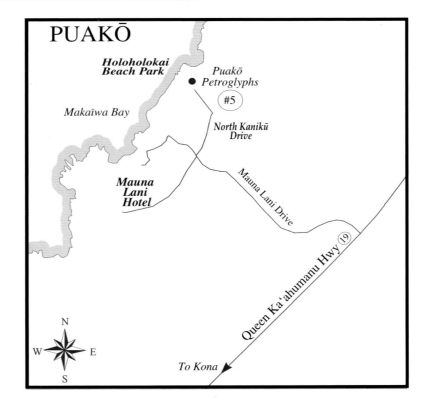

6. 'Anaeho'omalu Bay Petroglyphs, Kohala District-
Tales of ancient travelers

WHITE BEACHES, black lava, blue skies-visitors favor this beautiful coastline and come here to relax, swim, surf, play golf, and enjoy the many luxury resorts. The ancient *ali'i* also appreciated this area and came here to relax, fish, surf, and get away from all the pressures of being mighty warriors and chiefs. Many habitation sites and burial caves occupied the site of the present Royal Waikoloan Hotel, where a paved path with informational plaques leads to the remains of an ancient dwelling, a shrine, fishing gods, and two picturesque fishponds. The name 'Anaeho'omalu means "Protected Mullet," referring to the spring-fed fishponds, reserved for the use of *ali'i*, where fat mullet were raised. The ancient Hawaiians covered the opening to the fishponds with a grate that allowed small fish to enter from the ocean. Once inside the pond, the fish fed on algae and shrimp and became too fat to get back through the grate.

Island of Hawai'i

A footpath leads inland through the hotel's golf course to a huge, sun-baked petroglyph field. The field is on an ancient trail called the King's Highway, which travelers took when circling the island. The larger boundary sites have hundreds of petroglyphs, many of which were made by travelers. The trail probably afforded *kapu*-free crossings of district boundaries. Crossing district boundaries was a dangerous activity, as trespass was a serious offense. The petroglyphs may have been made to seek the protection of *'aumākua* in a strange land.

Many petroglyphs mark the birth of a child. The umbilical cord was placed in the *puka* and covered with *kapa* and a stone for protection. This enabled the child to absorb *mana* from the universe. If the *piko* was eaten by a rat, it was believed that the child would become a thief.

A few minutes walk south of 'Anaeho'omalu Bay, a narrow strip of sand leads to Kapalaoa Beach. This walk goes past numerous petroglyphs.

(Reference: Cox and Stasack 1970, 85.)

Stand in the fields at sunset and feel the mystery of the ancient carvings, some of the few pieces of ancient art in the world that are not in private or museum collections.

Directions: From Kailua-Kona, follow Highway 19 north for twenty-five miles. Turn left at the entrance to the Royal Waikoloan Hotel. A map is available at the King's Shops management office.

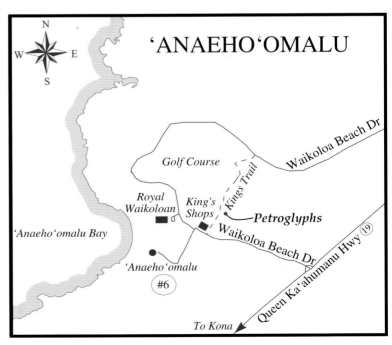

Ahu'ena Heiau, Kailua- Kona.
Note the golden plover on the
head of the god, Kōleamoku

7. Ahu'ena Heiau, Kailua-Kona-
Kamehameha I's seaside home

> *"These are my gods, whom I worship. Whether I do right or*
> *wrong I do not know. But I follow my faith, which cannot be*
> *wicked, as it commands me never to do wrong."*
> -Kamehameha I (James 1996, 15)

AHU'ENA HEIAU, its idols leering like fearsome sentinels, stands on
a stone platform built over the water at Kamakahonu (Eye of the
Turtle) on Kailua Bay. Ahu'ena (meaning "Burning Altar") was
initially a *luakini heiau*. It was later dedicated to Lono, god of
peace.

   Kamehameha the Great appreciated an ocean view. He
made his final home at this pretty cove in 1812 and maintained a
permanent residence here until his death seven years later. The
king also liked to fish. The waters around the *heiau* are filled with

large schools of fish, and giant marlin are caught in the deep waters of the bay.

The warrior king appears to have mellowed with age. During his years as a mighty conqueror, he worshiped his war god, Kū, and built *luakini heiau*. In his later years, however, he focused on Lono, god of peace and agriculture, who was worshiped particularly at the *makahiki* (harvest) ceremonies. Kamehameha I honored Lono by building Hale o Lono.

Kamehameha I wisely seized and held the gods of his enemies, and he displayed them as idols at Hale o Lono. He was extremely careful to secure for himself all the sorcery gods worshiped by the chiefs of the islands over which he ruled. He gave these gods their own houses and keepers. A chip of the powerful and feared *Kālaipāhoa*, or poisonwood god, from Moloka'i, was also stored in a god house. The king visited this god in the morning and evening and was said to eat a banana at the god's house while taking in the sweeping view of his plantations and the royal taro fields on Mt. Hualālai.

Kamehameha I ruled well and encouraged industry. He gained a knowledge of western ways and encouraged trading. He cooperated with foreigners but allowed no foreigner to buy land.

The *hale*, with its thatched houses and god images, was beautifully restored in the late 1970s under archaeological supervision. A French artist, Choris, sketched the temple when it still stood intact, and his sketch was used as a guide during rebuilding. The tallest *ki'i* (god image) is Kōleamoku, whose priests were experts in navigation. He is crowned with the golden plover, the type of bird said to have guided the first Polynesians to Hawai'i.

When the great king grew ill, the chief *kāhuna* advised him to build another *heiau* to his old war god, Kū. This was done, but the king was too weak to go to the *heiau*. The *kāhuna* suggested that a human sacrifice be offered for the king's life, but the king refused.

Dying, he whispered, "Enjoy quietly what I have made right." On May 8, 1819, Kamehameha the Great died. The kingdom was stunned and grief-stricken. Some chiefs requested that they be buried with him. Many people knocked out their front teeth in grief, and some tattooed the date on their bodies. The king's bones were stripped of flesh on the mortuary platform and prepared for burial. Hoapili, a *kahuna*, and one of the king's most

7. Ahu'ena Heiau

trusted *ali'i,* were entrusted to hide the bones. They are said to have been hidden in a cave and have never been found.

After Kamehameha's death, it was at this *heiau* that his son, Liholiho, reluctantly sat down with the strong-willed Queen Ka'ahumanu and his gentle mother, Queen Keōpūolani, and ate a meal on a formal occasion. The Hawaiian people were shocked at this public act of defiance-the ancient *kapu* of men eating with women had been broken. But no gods retaliated, and as a result the whole *kapu* system was overthrown.

Queen Keōpūolani declared, "Our gods have done us no good, they are cruel," and Hewahewa, the chief *kahuna,* said, "My thoughts have always been that there is one only great God, dwelling in the heavens."

Liholiho sent messengers to all the districts of Hawai'i ordering that *heiau* be destroyed and the images of gods be torn down.

(References: Kamakau 1992, 68; Kirch 1985, 166; Piercy 1992, 19; Richards 1825, 17; Stokes 1991, 43-47.)

Images guard Ahu'ena Heiau

The hills of the Kona District are riddled with large caves and lava tubes. We spoke to Dr. Yosihiko Sinoto, Senior Anthropologist at the Bishop Museum, who told us that in 1954 he went with a team from the museum to explore caves and lava tubes in Kona. He was invariably asked to lead the way, as he was the smallest. It was frightening going into the pitch-dark tubes, and the thought of being underground during an

Island of Hawai'i

earthquake was often on his mind. To his horror, while the team was in a mile-long lava tube the ground began to shake. He ran to the side of the tube and fell to the floor as rocks tumbled to the ground around him. It seemed a very long few minutes before the earthquake stopped.

Many treasure seekers have attempted to locate Kamehameha's burial site somewhere in these dark caves.

Directions: The *heiau* is on the waterfront in Kailua-Kona, on the grounds of the King Kamehameha Kona Beach Hotel. The hotel offers a self-guided tour. Nearby is Hawai'i's first Christian church, Moku'aikaua Church, built in 1823. The original building was a grass hut, and the beautiful lava-and-coral church was built in 1837.

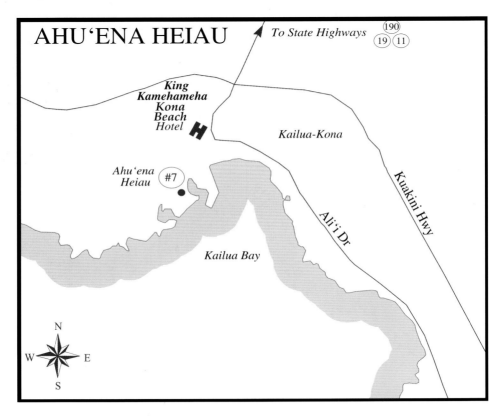

7. Ahu'ena Heiau

Ku'emanu Heiau, the surfer's temple

8. Ku'emanu Heiau, Kahalu'u Bay, Kona District– *Surfers' temple*

> *The great sea from Kahiki*
> *Quietly surrounds the island;*
> *The sea breaks on the reef flats.*
> *The sea whispers to the pebbles;*
> *The hair is dressed with seawater,*
> *The hair is reddened by the salty sea,*
> *The hair is yellowed by the foamy sea.*
> -Hawaiian chant (Kamakau 1991, 44)

SMOOTH, ROLLING breakers, tall men and women on long wooden boards: the ancient Hawaiians invented the sport of surfing, and Ku'emanu Heiau was dedicated to this chiefly art. The main platform gives an excellent view of the rolling waves in Kahalu'u Bay. Here, surfers of long ago prayed for good surf as they sat on

Island of Hawai'i

the terraces and watched the waves. They used the freshwater pool to remove salt from their boards-some customs never change! The *heiau* is pleasant, with its swaying palm trees and view of the sparkling ocean, although there is an ominous touch at the north end of the *heiau*, where there is a bone pit associated with *luakini heiau*.

When the surf was up, whole villages would drop everything to ride the waves. The most sought after wave was a high, smooth wave that did not break all at once. Surfers used chants to call up the surf when it was small. Hawaiian chiefs rode magnificent, long boards, some measuring as much as fifteen feet. The longest surfboard in the Bishop Museum is sixteen feet in length and made of *koa*. Commoners rode boards of six to seven feet in length. Before choosing a tree from which to make a board, a surfer would offer a red *kūmū* fish to the gods. After the board was made, it was dedicated with a special prayer.

Kalamakua-a-Kaipūhōlua was a popular and good chief who loved to surf. One day, as he worked in his fields, he heard his men shouting and cheering.

"What is the shouting from the seashore?" he asked.

"It's a skilled woman surfer," was the reply.

Kalamakua-a-Kaipūhōlua ran to the shore and saw the beautiful Kelea-nui-noho expertly riding the waves, her long hair flying in the wind. When she reached the shore she stood up, naked. The chief wrapped his shoulder-covering around her and took her to a *kapu* place. They married. Their children became the rulers of Maui and Hawai'i.

Today there are still offerings on this altar-perhaps surfers still pray here for the perfect wave.

(References: Kalākaua 1990, 245; Kamakau 1991, 45-49, 50, 86; Pukui, Elbert, and Mookini 1989, 120; Stokes 1991, 67-70.)

"Make certain," said Buddy Peters, a Hawaiian friend, "that you always enter a heiau by the correct entrance. It's safer. That way the spirits know you come in peace. Enter politely, like you would want someone to enter your own home. If someone climbs through your window, you're not going to like it!"

8. Ku'emanu Heiau

Altar of the heiau – photo credit State Parks Division, DLNR

Directions: From Kailua-Kona, follow Aliʻi Drive south for about five miles. The *heiau* is oceanside of Aliʻi Drive beside St. Peter's Catholic Church, "The Little Blue Church." The church is built over part of the *heiau*, the *kāhuna* residence, a common practice in those times. The seven-mile stretch of coast here was considered one of the most sacred places on Hawaiʻi; there are burial caves, remains of *heiau*, fields where bloody battles took place, and many stories of ghosts. On the lighter side, nearby Kahaluʻu Beach Park is a great place to snorkel and swim with turtles.

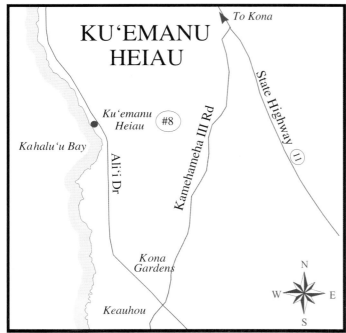

KU'EMANU HEIAU

To Kona

Kuʻemanu Heiau #8

Kahaluʻu Bay

Aliʻi Dr

Kamehameha III Rd

State Highway 11

Kona Gardens

Keauhou

N W E S

Ho'okala gives shaka at fish shrine, Keauhou Archaeological Complex

9. Keauhou Archaeological Complex, Kona District-*Heiau, fish gods, fertility*

THE GROUNDS of the Outrigger Keauhou Beach Resort are sacred lands and contain three *heiau,* the King's Pond, fish gods, and petroglyphs.

Ke'ekū Heiau was an imposing structure, but it has been damaged over the centuries by the surf of stormy seas. Some remaining walls of the *heiau* are eleven feet high and more than thirty feet wide. There is a narrow entrance from the beach on the south. This was a *luakini heiau,* and Kamalālāwalu of Maui was beheaded and sacrificed here when he failed in his attempt to conquer the island of Hawai'i. The spirits of his black-and-white dogs are said to stand on the temple platform, still waiting for their master. A petroglyph of Chief Kamalālāwalu can be seen at low tide just offshore at the southwest end of the Keauhou complex. The petroglyph depicts a powerful man, and it does look as if he is depicted without his head.

Hāpaiali'i (Pregnant Chiefess) Heiau was constructed on top of a lava flow at the water's edge. It is interesting to note the size and regularity of the great lava blocks. The 3,900-foot break-water is said to have been constructed with the help of supernatural powers.

Kapuʻanoni Heiau was a fishing temple. Next to it is a sacred bathing tide pool for royalty. Nearby are two stone fish gods brought by canoe from Maui. They watch over and guard the King's Pond and curse anyone who takes fish from the pond. There is also a fertility pit for those desirous of a child. (References: Emory, McCoy, and Barrere 1971, 16-19; Stokes 1991, 71-79.)

We met a man named Hoʻokala at the fish god shrine. His white coral-shell lei looked striking against his tanned skin. He told us that he likes to dive for lobster at night.

"Aren't you afraid of sharks?" I asked.

"No," he smiled. "The shark is my family ʻaumakua. But I also take a forty-four mag bullet-bang stick with a light, just in case he doesn't recognize me."

Directions: The complex is located on the grounds of the Outrigger Keauhou Beach Resort, 78-6740 Aliʻi Drive, Kailua-Kona. The hotel offers cultural tours; call cultural director for times and days; (808) 322-3441. Note the abandoned Lagoon Hotel adjacent to the fishpond and Keʻekū Heiau. It is said to be haunted.

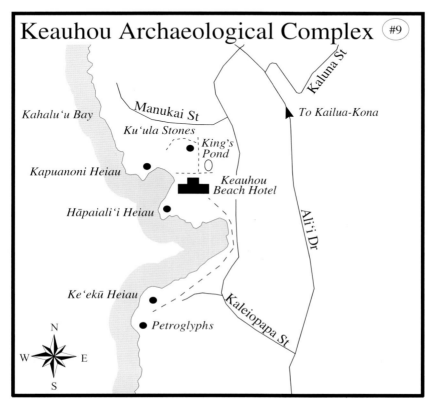

Keauhou Archaeological Complex #9

Hikiau Heiau - Capt. Cook was venerated here as the God Lono

10. Hikiau Heiau and Ka'awaloa Village, Kona District-
Where Captain Cook was killed

Behold Lono places the stars
That sail through the heavens.
High resplendent is the great image of Lono.
-Hawaiian chant (Beckwith 1970, 31)

IN 1779 the Hawaiians living in villages around Kealakekua Bay saw an astonishing sight: as prophesied, the god Lono arrived on his "floating island." Two British ships, the *H.M.S. Resolution* and *Discovery*, their tall white sails billowing, sailed into the bay.

The Hawaiians were celebrating the *makahiki*, or harvest season. This season praised Lono, the god of farming and fertility, who returned ritually each year to bring the Kona rains so essential for the growth of crops. The *kāhuna* of Lono wore white *kapa* garments, similar to the sails of the ships.

Captain Cook, the world-famous explorer arriving on the *H.M.S. Resolution,* was thought to be the actual incarnation of the god Lono coming at last to bless the people. Fifteen hundred canoes rowed into the bay to greet him. Fascinating old pen-and-ink sketches at the Bishop Museum show canoes carrying *kāhuna.* These priests, their heads covered by gourds with black, gaping holes for eyes, are cradling god images. Cook, as Lono incarnate, was taken to the Hikiau Heiau platform while *kāhuna* chanted prayers and the crowd cried out "O Lono!" The *heiau* is of the *luakini* type and Cook would have seen many *ki'i* glaring at him as he ascended the platform.

For the weeks that the ships were anchored in the bay, the British were treated as gods. But the Hawaiians noted the sailors' enthusiastic behavior with the free-spirited, sexually obliging Hawaiian women and began to doubt their godlike status.

Cook left the islands with his ships loaded with supplies. Unfortunately, a storm broke at sea, and a cracked mast caused him to return to Kealakekua Bay. This time he was greeted with suspicion. It was not the custom of the god Lono to return twice. The behavior of the sailors had been noted with disapproval, and the crew had also eaten an enormous amount of food.

The Hawaiians stole a rowboat, and Cook decided to take Chief Kalani'opu'u hostage on board his ship until the rowboat was returned. The elderly chief, warned by his favorite wife, was unwilling to go with Cook. A crowd of three thousand Hawaiians gathered to defend their chief, and Cook was killed in the resulting melee. A white obelisk across the bay from the *heiau,* erected by the British government, marks the place where Captain Cook fell.

Captain Cook's body was sacrificed to Kū. It was defleshed, and the bones were carefully wrapped in the manner accorded to a chief's bones. Tradition says that Cook's remains were ritually carried to *makahiki* ceremonies around the island. Some say that his liver and heart were accidentally eaten by children who thought they were the remains of a dog.

Hikiau Heiau was originally more than 250 feet long and over 100 feet wide. The walls are carved into the *pali,* and the western corner is sixteen feet high. The platform was meticulously filled with small, smooth stones. A *lele* altar has been erected on the platform, and when we visited, it held lei offerings and bananas wrapped in *ti* leaves.

Altar of the heiau

The village of Ka'awaloa, where Cook was slain, lies nearby, covered by trees and undergrowth. Stone walls and platforms are visible from the narrow dirt road that descends down to the coast. Caves in the cliffs are the secret burial places of chiefs. (References: Beckwith 1970, 31; Bisignani 1994, 26-28; Kamakau 1991, 98-104; Kirch 1985, 164-66; Sahlins 1981, 20-22.)

We spoke to Fern Kalehuamakanoe Pule, an interesting kupuna, who recited the names of her ancestors back to Hewahewa, the famous kahuna who predicted the exact location where strangers would arrive on the shores of Hawai'i. He foretold the fall of the kingdom.

10. Hikiau Heiau and Ka'awaloa Village

We were very impressed by her famous ancestor, but she smiled and said that her mother had always told her not to brag about being ali'i. If you did that in the old days, another ali'i would come and knock you off.

She chanted for us in a beautiful, low voice and told us that when she had chanted at the birth site of Kamehameha III, her companion had seen a procession of chiefs and warriors marching toward them. "Be quiet," she'd been told. "Your chants are waking the dead."

Directions: From Kailua-Kona, follow Highway 11 about twelve miles south, and turn right on Nāpō'opo'o Road. At the intersection of Middle Ke'ei Road, turn right and head toward the ocean. Turn into Nāpō'opo'o Beach Park. The *heiau* is at the southern end of Kealakekua Bay. Across the bay, you can see the white monument commemorating the death of Captain Cook. The water at the monument is clear and teems with fish and coral and, sometimes, dolphins and sharks. Commercial dive boats visit the site from Keauhou, and nearby stores rent out kayaks.

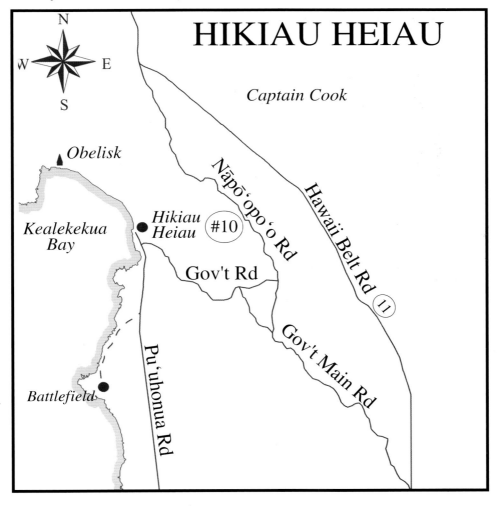

HIKIAU HEIAU

N · W · E · S

Captain Cook

Obelisk

Hikiau Heiau #10

Kealekekua Bay

Gov't Rd

Nāpō'opo'o Rd

Hawaii Belt Rd 11

Gov't Main Rd

Battlefield

Pu'uhonua Rd

Hale o Keawe Heiau, mausoleum for royal bones

11. Pu'uhonua o Hōnaunau, Kona District-
Place of refuge

MAKE SURE that you see this beautiful, historic park and experience its peaceful *mana*. This perfect cove, its tall palms planted as beacons, was a welcome sight to breakers of *kapu* and to defeated warriors. Pu'uhonua o Hōnaunau was a sanctuary, a place of refuge.

In ancient Hawai'i, people's lives were governed by the *kapu* system. The number of laws to be obeyed was daunting, and the penalty for disobeying a law was often death. Death was the penalty for eating with your husband or wife or allowing your shadow to fall on an *ali'i* or his food. Historian David Malo wrote that "when a *tabu* chief ate, the people in his presence must kneel, and if anyone raised his knee from the ground, he was put to death. If any man put forth in a *kioloa* [a long, swift racing canoe] at the same time as the *tabu* chief, the penalty was death." *Kapu* breakers were pursued, as their deeds could cause the fearsome gods to punish everyone with lava flows or tidal waves.

It was like a terrible game of life-or-death for a fugitive to get inside the ten-foot-high walls of the place of refuge. *Kapu* breakers could run over land or swim across the bay into the sanctuary, but while they were outside the walls, they could be sacrificed by a variety of horrible means, including burning, stoning, drowning, clubbing, or strangulation. Once inside the walls, they were in a safe haven with a garden, a fresh-water spring, coconut palms, and a bay filled with fish. There is even a stone marked for games of *kōnane* (checkers). *Kāhuna* performed cleansing rituals and restored *mana*, and once cleansed, the *kapu* breaker could leave safely, protected by the gods.

Fierce Kiʻi (images) at the Hale o Keawe

Kaʻahumanu, the favorite wife of Kamehameha I, sought refuge here once, swimming miles across the bay and hiding behind a large stone that is now called Kaʻahumanu's Stone. She had offended the mighty king, not an unusual event for this six-foot-tall, beautiful young woman whose very body the longsuffering king had declared *kapu* in an effort to control her. This *kapu* meant that her lovers faced death if discovered, and some paid this ultimate price. This did not deter the queen from taking others. In this instance, the queen's small dog barked and betrayed her hiding place to Kamehameha, but he forgave his wayward young wife.

The overwhelming sanctity of the site came from the spiritual *mana* of the *aliʻi* buried here. Hale o Keawe contained the bones of twenty-three *aliʻi*, ancestors of Kamehameha I. The bones were later removed to a secret burial place, but some of the *mana* remains. Offerings are still seen at the *heiau*.

Hale o Keawe is completely reconstructed in accordance with old records and vintage sketches. Traditional tools were used to carve the ferocious, large idols who guard the *heiau*. Trails lead to burial sites, an ancient village, the royal fish pond, and a *kōnane* game chiseled on a rock.

This place of refuge was constructed around the year 1550. It is interesting to note that Hawaiians were not the only people who constructed cities of refuge-in the Old Testament of the Bible, when the Hebrews entered the promised land Joshua followed a directive given by God through Moses and named six Hebrew cities of refuge. The cities were all built on high ground so that fugitives could see them.
(References: Kirch 1985, 161-64; Kirch 1996, 109-10; Pukui, Elbert, and Mookini 1989, 10, 38.)

This is a place of peace and healing. William "Pila" Chiles, healer, Huna teacher, and writer, relates that he has been taking terminally ill people here for healing since 1986. He recommends going at sunset. Officially the park is closed, but you are allowed to remain until midnight. The place with the most healing energy, Pila says, is at the point that protrudes into the ocean in front of the Hale o Keawe. A small ki'i is standing there. He looks rather aroused, but remember that sexual energy is a force of creation, and this is a place where vigor returns. Pila tells his patients to take a deep breath and ponder what needs to be released from their lives. They are advised to give up what they want to be rid of with each expired breath, in a ritualistic manner. The subconscious mind likes ritual. Then, say "Mahalo" (thank you), he advises, and your subconscious mind will consider it done.
(Reference: Chiles 1992.)

The Great Wall separating the royal compound from the place of refuge

11. *Pu'uhonua o Hōnaunau*

Directions: From Kailua-Kona, follow Highway 11 south to Highway 160 turn right and proceed to the south shore of Hōnaunau Bay. This is a very interesting, historical sanctuary that offers self-guided walking tours, a visitor center, wheelchair accessible areas, and a pretty picnic area near a cove under shady trees. Just beyond the visitor center, an 1871 trail leads to Ki'ilae Village ruins, remains of a heiau, a hōlua (slide), and a lava tube. Park tel. (808) 328-2288. Entrance fee: $2 adults. An informative brochure is available at the entrance.

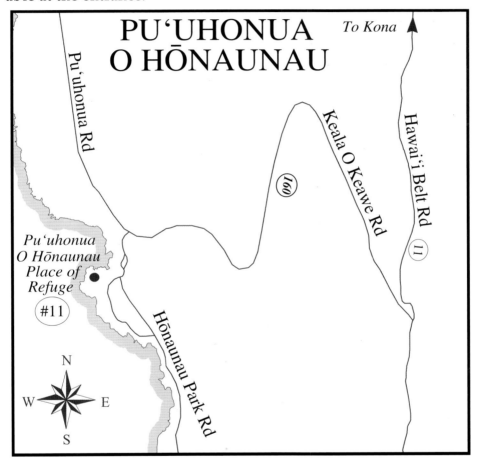

Island of Hawai'i

Bamboo fishing poles offered at Kalalea Heiau

12. Kalalea Heiau,
Ka'ū, South Point-
Power vortex, lava tubes

KA'Ū IS one of the domains of the goddess Pele, *wahine kapu*, where anything can happen. The forces of nature and the volatile goddess wield a lot of power. The area is unstable and subject to large earthquakes, tsunami, and volcanic eruptions. In 1868, the largest earthquake ever recorded in the Hawaiian Islands (7.5 on the Richter scale) hit Ka'ū. The coastline subsided six feet, and a tsunami destroyed villages, burying a village of thirty-one people. Five days later, Mauna Loa erupted. Jets of steam and smoke went up from many points, and four distinct streams of lava rushed down the mountain.

In 1975, another huge quake occurred. The coast again subsided, more than ten feet this time, and generated a tsunami. No wonder the Hawaiians felt that the gods needed to be placated!

Windswept South Point is the southernmost tip of the United States, and it is considered by many, including *Huna* teacher William 'Pila' Chiles, to be a power vortex, a "doorway" to the other side. He considers it, like the Bermuda Triangle, to be "some sort of rip in the fabric of time" (Chiles 1992). The iron ore content of the earth here is so dense that space shuttles use this point to reorient their instruments whenever they lose contact with Earth.

There are many stories of UFO sightings here, and Ka'ū resident Miriam Baker has built a UFO landing strip. Miriam told us some of her experiences, which were very interesting! She originally owned a business in Alaska. Angels helped her make the business a success, so when she sold it for $250,000, she dedicated 40 percent of the proceeds to building an angel park in Ka'ū. Then neighbors told her that they had seen UFOs trying to land at the angel park, but they'd flown off, probably because the lava made a bad landing field. Miriam covered a large area with macadamia nut shells to create a smooth landing strip. She has not yet been visited by UFOs but hopes that she will be. She says the park is open to anyone except bigots and boozers.

Miriam came to Ka'ū because of the energy force here-she calls it a "stepping stone to heaven." She told us that she is in constant communication with angels and that anyone can access them, but you have to first recognize your own divinity. Angels mostly help you when you are trying to help others, and if you make a list of what you want to do for others in private, the angels will help you reach your goals.

Thousands of lava tubes riddle the area, many of which were used as burial caves. Some of the huge chambers were used by ancient Hawaiians as hospices for the seriously ill. Lose contact with the troubles of the world, and seek yourself in the pitch black and totally silent tubes, but don't get lost! Watch which way you go, as Hawaiians also believed South Point to be a "doorway" to the hereafter, a "leaping place of souls."

Kula Kai Caverns, several miles of fascinating braided lava tubes, snake their way under the convoluted lava fields of Ka'ū. We explored this world under Hawai'i with Ric Elhard, the adventurous present guardian of the caves. Here Pele, the goddess of fire, has decorated thirty-foot-high caverns with lacey drapes of crystals and curtains of pale, alienlike roots. There are swirls

Island of Hawai'i

of luscious chocolate and delicate, pointed stalactites.

Archaeology surveys show that the Kula Kai Caverns were not used as burial chambers, but as shelters. Hawaiians on forays from coastal areas rested here and obtained water from this underground source. Ric, crawling into unsurveyed lava tubes, identified with these travelers from long ago who ventured several hundred or even a thousand feet into the dark reaches of the tubes to place gourds under the dripping water. He pictured them as they held burning branches for torches and wiggled through the last coffinlike sections to get the very smallest amount of liquid.

"True dedication. True warriors," he commented, and then he was enveloped with cold chicken skin.

"Hey! Did you feel that?" his fellow spelunker called. "They're here, brah."

Kalalea Heiau, on the headland at the farthermost point of South Point, is a fishing shrine. Within the *heiau* is a large stone named after Kū'ula, the god of fishermen, where fishermen con-

At left: dramatic cliffs at South Point, below: altar platform at Kalalea Heiau

12. Kalalea Heiau

ducted ceremonies and left offerings, usually the first fish of the catch. Branch coral, bamboo fishing poles, and fishhooks are offered here today.
(References: Kirch 1985, 158-59; Stokes 1991, 115-19.)

Directions: Follow Highway 11 south until the turnoff to South Point, between the 69 and 70-mile markers, about six miles before Nāʻālehu. A narrow paved road drops south twelve miles to South Point and Kalalea Heiau. At the coast, when the road splits, go right. Beware of high seas at the tip.

    The turnoff on Kula Kai Road oceanside to Kula Kai Caverns is between the 77- and 78-mile markers. Proceed to the ninth street, where you will see the visitor hut on your right.

    To tour the caves contact: Kula Kai Caverns, Kaʻū. Tel. (808) 929-7539. E-mail Caver@kulakaicaverns.com.

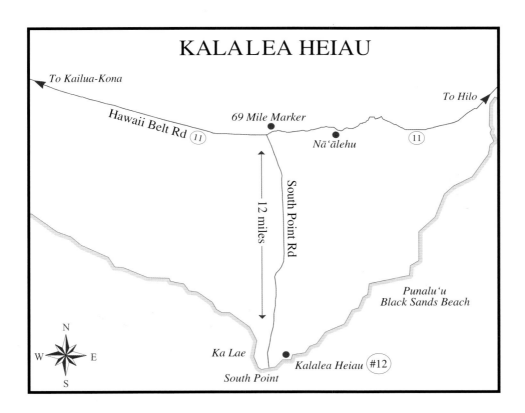

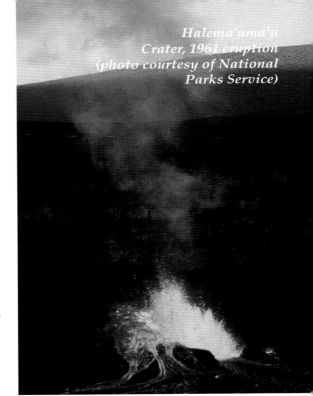

13. Kīlauea Volcano, Kaʻū-Home of Pele, *Goddess of fire*

Jets of lava gushed from Kahiki.
Pele hurled her lightning,
vomit of flame, outpouring of lava
was the woman's farewell.
-Hawaiian chant (Pukui and Korn 1973, 55)

Hawaiʻi Volcanoes National Park, with its wisps of vapor, smell of sulfur, huge desolate craters, and shiny fields of black lava, is the domain of Pele, the very active Hawaiian goddess of fire. The powerful forces of nature are obvious here, and Pele's *mana* is strong. She is still actively worshiped.

Pele has an exciting and fascinating dwelling place. Halemaʻumaʻu Crater, home of the fiery goddess, is twelve hundred feet deep and more than two miles in circumference. Hot steam rises from the crater, and you can feel the power trapped under the surface. When Pele is in residence, this crater springs into life, lava boils, and fountains of lava glow in the night.

In ancient times, *kāhuna* made offerings at Uwēkāhuna (Wailing Priest) Bluff. The fiery goddess needed to be constantly appeased. Today offerings still line the banks of the crater: rocks wrapped in ti leaves, leis, bananas, even bottles of gin. George Lycurgus, who managed the Volcano House in the 1890s, always left bottles of gin for the goddess, so that she would favor him and his guests with a lava eruption.

Ancient Hawaiians thought it very desirable to have an ancestor who was one of Pele's fiery spirits. One way to achieve this was to offer the ancestor's bones to the goddess by wrapping them in *kapa* and dropping them into the crater. Historian Mary Kawena Pukui related that her great grandmother's body had been offered in this manner. The flesh was removed from her bones, and the family chanted, prayed, and let her bones go happily to her "people," who were fire.

Chain of Craters Road winds twenty miles down to the coast, where Kīlauea Volcano sends an endless stream of red-hot lava into the sea. Huge clouds of steam form over the cliffs when the two-thousand-degree lava hits the water. The sight is particularly impressive at sunset.

Pele's domain is full of strange sights and places to explore. One of the world's weirdest walks is a trail constructed by prisoners across the steaming floor of Kīlauea. A walk through Thurston Lava Tube is dark and mysterious as it winds under the lava field. Another area has steaming yellow sulfur banks and steam vents. An interesting petroglyph trail at the 16-mile marker contains thousands of petroglyphs.

(References: Ching and Stephens 1994; Kirch 1985, 33; Pukui, Haertig, and Lee 1972, 2: 126; Hawai'i Volcanoes National Park Pamphlet, 1999.)

The goddess Pele has a volcanic personality. She is unpredictable-sometimes furious, sometimes loving. Many people say that they have seen the goddess; appearing either as an old woman, or as a young girl. There are many stories of sightings before volcanic eruptions.

Island lore tells that the power of the goddess extends beyond the shores of Hawai'i. When Charles Bishop, the co-founder of the Bernice P. Bishop Estate, left Hawai'i to settle in California, the enraged Pele stalked him, causing the earthquake of 1906. The fire that resulted from that earthquake and destroyed much of San Francisco was said to have had the unmistakable brand of Pele.

Mary Kawena Pukui wrote that the lava stones of Pele were so filled with power that they could be dangerous. Each year more than two thousand pounds of lava rocks are returned to Hawai'i Volcanoes National Park, accompanied by letters of apology from all over the world. They are written by people who have taken lava from Pele's domain and have experienced "Pele's curse." A ranger told us that the sheer bulk of letters and stones is overwhelming, and some even come with notes like "please return to the 55-mile marker" (a lava field that is nearly thirty miles away from the visitor center). Here is one such letter to Hawai'i Volcanoes National Park:

Dear Sir or Madam,
Enclosed you will find what has become the biggest mistake we ever made. We ask the goddess, Pele, for forgiveness, to forgive our arrogance in thinking we could hold her raw, chaotic, elemental power. We ask that peace and harmony be restored to our lives in returning these to her.

Directions: Hawai'i Volcanoes National Park is thirty miles southwest of Hilo on Highway 11. Within the park are a hotel with a huge fireplace and a dining room with a panoramic view, cabins, camping, scenic driving, hiking, a museum, a visitor center, and wheelchair accessible areas. The flowing lava is best viewed at sunset, at the end of Chain of Craters Road. Check at the visitor center for an update on volcanic activity. Take binoculars and don't go off the trail; people have died here. For information, call (808) 985-6000. Entrance fee: $10 per vehicle for a 7-day pass. An informative brochure is provided at the entrance.

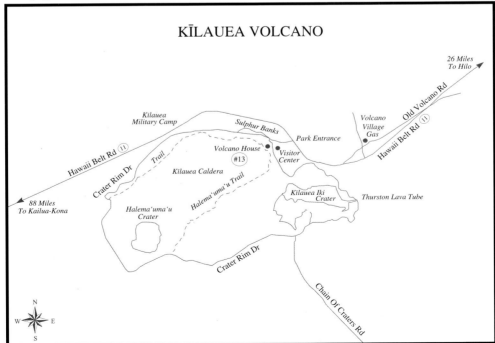

Dreaded Waha'ula Heiau
(photo courtesy of State Parks Division, DLNR)

14. Waha'ula Heiau, Puna-
First and bloodiest temple to Kū

> Shudder at what lies behind you;
> Shudder at what has gone by;
> Shudder at what lies before you –
> Maori Chant - Morrill 1969, 107

EVEN PELE, the volatile goddess of fire, respected the *mana* of Waha'ula Heiau. In A.D. 1200, 1450, and 1983, Kīlauea Volcano erupted with massive flows of molten lava but the *heiau* remained untouched. In 1983, hundreds of homes and the $1.2 million National Park Visitor Center were destroyed, but the lava stopped inches from the base of the massive stone walls of Waha'ula Heiau. Hawaiians and non-Hawaiians alike said that Pele had spared the *heiau*.

This *heiau* was the first and one of the most horrific sacrificial temples dedicated by the Tahitian high priest Pā'ao to the war god, Kū. It was also the last to be destroyed after the abolition of the *kapu* system in 1819. Its name means "red or sore mouth," as its altar consumed many victims. Even the smoke from the *heiau* was sacred, so that anyone passing under its shadow would be put

Island of Hawai'i

to death. If the smoke drifted over a specific family's house and victims were needed, the entire family was liable to be sacrificed.

The *Mū*, whose job it was to collect people for sacrifice, would go in groups of three at night, eavesdropping on houses to find anyone breaking the *kapu*. If these body catchers found no one to sacrifice, sometimes priests became the victims.

Since 1983, lava flows have dramatically changed the landscape, so there's no guarantee the *heiau* will be there when you visit, or that you will be allowed by park rangers to hike to it. An older structure is buried by lava. As of 1997, only part of the *heiau* reconstructed during the time of Kamehameha I was left, a submerged temple standing on the only *kīpuka* (an island of older lava in a sea of new lava).

(References: Kamakau 1991, 97-100; Kirch 1985, 259; Stokes 1991, 136-44.)

A model was made of the heiau in the 1930's, using stones from the Waha'ula Heiau. It was placed on exhibit in the Bishop Museum.

The mother of a young man working at the museum had a dream predicting danger for her son. She warned him not to go to work, but the young man felt obligated to attend to his job. That day, as he was repairing the lofty roof of the building, he fell to his death, plunging through a skylight and landing on the heiau. Hawaiians said that the model heiau had claimed its first victim.

The scale model of this luakini heiau is still on display in the Bishop Museum's Hawaiian Hall. A ferocious six-foot-high statue of Kū looms over it.

Directions: Ask the park ranger at the visitor's center for the latest information on whether it is possible to access this site. Tel.: (808) 985-6000. From Hawai'i Volcanoes National Park, follow Chain of Craters Road to the road's end. Remains of the *heiau* are a seven-mile hike from the end of Chain of Craters Road.

14. Waha'ula Heiau

15. Naha Stone, Hilo– *The Excalibur story of Hawai'i*

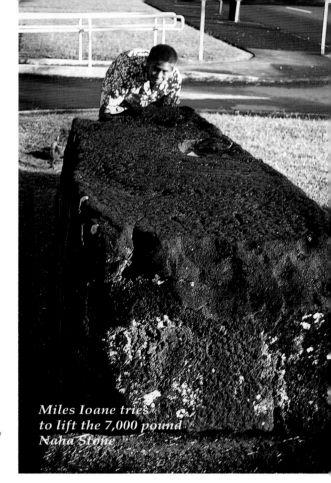

Miles Ioane tries to lift the 7,000 pound Naha Stone.

This seven-thousand-pound lava stone, sacred to the ruling *Naha ali'i*, was brought from Kaua'i by canoe. The stone was *kapu* to anyone who was not of the *Naha* line, and it was believed to be able to detect if a baby was a part of the *naha* line. A true baby of the *Naha* line would lie quietly when placed on the stone; other babies would cry. The *Naha* stone and the large stone beside it were part of Pinao Heiau.

Many years before the birth of Kamehameha the Great, a powerful *kahuna* prophesied that the man who moved the *Naha* stone would be the greatest king of Hawai'i. When he was only fourteen years old, the ambitious Kamehameha I, who was already six feet tall and strong, decided to move the stone. The kahuna Kalaniwahine had told him that he would have to overthrow a mountain before he would conquer the Hawaiian Islands, and this seemed a similar feat.

Kamehameha chose the time of the *makahiki* festival, a time of peace, as the safest time to try to move the stone. As he was not of the Naha line of *ali'i*, if he tried to move the stone and failed, it could result in his death. Lono was a good-natured god, not a man-eating god like Kū, but his *kāhuna* were also likely to drown or beat to death anyone who broke the *kapu* of the stone.

Hundreds of people gathered at the *makahiki* festival. At night, the *kāhuna* kept burning torches and *kukui* nut lamps by the stone, and they kept watch over it all day, so Kamehameha had no chance to practice moving it. It would be a day of death or fame. On the chosen day he went up to the massive rock and pushed and struggled to lift it. Nothing happened. He placed his shoulders under it and heaved. He moved the rock, then he lifted it and turned it over. As the prophet had foretold, Kamehameha I became Hawai'i 's greatest king.
(References: McBride 1969, 34; James 1996, 53-54.)

Directions: The stone is located in front of the Hilo Public Library, 300 Wai'ānuenue Avenue. Most restaurants in Hilo have a pamphlet titled "Discover Downtown Hilo, A Walking Tour of Historic Sites."

We recommend taking a side trip from Hilo to 'Akaka Falls, a beautiful 422-foot waterfall surrounded by exquisite tropical gardens. Ceremonies were performed here to honor the god Kanaloa, and the large stone above the falls, Pōhaku o Kāloa, is named for his special nights. Take Highway 19 north to Honomū, twelve miles from Hilo, and turn left. 'Akaka Falls Park is located three miles from Honomū at the end of Route 220.

'Akaka Falls

Coconut Island at dawn connected by footbridge to Lili'uokalani Gardens

16. Coconut Island (Mokuola), Hilo-
Place of healing

"You have almost landed at the Isle of Life."
-Hawaiian saying (Clark 1985, 18)

MOKUOLA (ISLAND of Life and Healing) is a little island reached by footbridge from outside Lili'uokalani Gardens. In ancient Hawai'i, the island was famous for its curative spring waters. Near the old landing is a small sea pool called Pua'akāheka, also a special healing spot.

Some of the healing required the active participation of the sick person. *Kāhuna lapa'au* promised healing for those able to swim around one of the rocks at the eastern inlet. Anyone who could swim three times around the island underwater was assured of a long life.

The island was also a place of refuge in ancient times. Breakers of *kapu* laws and vanquished warriors were safe at this pretty place. They could make offerings and leave as free men,

Island of Hawai'i

Coconut Island, island of healing and place of refuge

protected by the *mana* of the gods.

The island was full of *mana*, and umbilical cords (*piko*) were placed under rocks to gain power for babies and the protection of the goddess Hina.
(Reference: Pukui, Elbert, and Mookini 1989, 156.)

Directions: In Hilo on Banyan Drive at the intersection of Lahiwai Street, cross to the island over a footbridge in front of the lovely grounds of the Hilo Hawaiian Hotel.

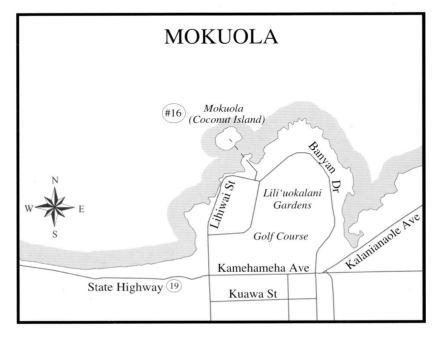

16. Coconut Island

Cinder cone and surreal landscape at Mauna Kea Volcano

17. Mauna Kea Volcano, Hāmākua District- *Where worlds collide*

> *"The idea of a sacred place … is apparently as old as life itself."*
> -Joseph Campbell

MAUNA KEA (White Mountain), a mighty, ancient volcano, was the home of Poliʻahu, the snow goddess. The mountain, at 13,796 feet above sea level, is the highest point in all of Polynesia. It has special significance, as Hawaiians considered it to be the "gateway to heaven." *Kāhuna* climbed to this far and lofty summit to be nearer to the divine creator.

High places have been used since early times for spiritual communion with the gods. The most sacred places on the Hawaiian Islands are the highest mountain peaks; these are Mount Waiʻaleʻale on Kauaʻi, Mount Kaʻala on Oʻahu, Mount Haleakalā on Maui, and Mauna Kea on Hawaiʻi. These peaks exhibit bizarre

Island of Hawaiʻi

extremes; Mauna Kea, when measured from the seabed, is the world's highest mountain, measuring 32,000 feet. Mount Wai'ale'ale is the wettest place on earth, and Mount Haleakalā is the world's largest dormant volcano.

The higher elevations of Hawai'i's mountains contain shrines, sacred rocks, and many secret burial sites where bones of *ali'i* were placed for safekeeping. Some Hawaiians believe that these sanctuaries and spiritual places have been violated by the construction of observatories, and resistance to further development is strong.

The clear, chilly air of Mauna Kea's summit makes this one of the world's premier locations for astronomers. Shiny domes of observatories cluster on top of the mountain, creating a science-fiction landscape. Nations from around the world have come here to build some of the most powerful telescopes in the world. Keck, a superscope with a thirty-three-foot-wide viewing surface, has a unique multi-mirrored system, making it look like the eye of a giant science-fiction bug. Japan's supertelescope, the Subaru, a $300 million project, has produced remarkably clear images of deep space, including images of the most distant quasar known, about fourteen billion light years away. On Mauna Kea, scientists can look back to the beginning of time and watch stars being born.

Is this a place of strange energy? Saddle Road, the winding road that leads to Mauna Kea, is known for sightings of night marchers and UFOs.
(References: Kirch 1985, 134, 180; Pukui, Elbert, and Mookini 1989, 148.)

We received permission to visit the University of Hawai'i Observatory on Mauna Kea and drove to the residences just below the peak, where we were met by a student of the university's astronomy department. Scientists from all over the world apply years in advance to stay here and use the telescopes.

We needed a four-wheel-drive vehicle to travel to the summit; the road is steep and winding. The view is panoramic and surreal. Small craters surrounding the volcano resemble inverted ice cream cones with snow packed into dark brown cones. The air is icy, and we were glad we brought heavy jackets. A gale was blowing at the summit, and winds whipped around the silver observatories. It seemed almost possible to raise our arms and fly over the pristine snow-covered craters.

At this high altitude the air is thin, and it is inadvisable to stay

17. Mauna Kea Volcano

too long at the summit until you have become acclimatized. Children under the age of fourteen are advised not to visit the summit, as the lack of oxygen can do damage to their brains.

Shiny domes of observatories cluster on the summit of Mauna Kea

We were fortunate enough to see inside one of the observatories. The telescope was massive—a huge black funnel peering out into space. It projects images onto television screens. A scientist was looking at a screen depicting an outer galaxy, and the little dots of stars had a red tinge. They were very, very far away, both in distance and in time. It was truly amazing to be viewing a galaxy billions of light years away.

As we drove on, the Waimea fog surrounded us, and the possibility of night marchers or UFOs seemed very real.

Directions: Take the Saddle Road, Highway 200, inland from Hilo by continuing out Wai'ānuenue Avenue. Turn right after about 23 miles at Mauna Kea Road and continue ten miles to the observatories. The visitor center is at 9,200 feet above sea level. The area is subject to snowstorms in winter. Tours of the University of Hawai'i's telescope are given Saturdays and Sundays—call (808) 961-2180 for information.

Beautiful Waipi'o Valley
coastline from Waipi'o Lookout

18. Waipi'o Valley, Hāmākua District- *Home of the night marchers*

> *Famous is my home, beloved Waipi'o,*
> *And the beautiful fringes of the land,*
> *A castle, a royal residence. . . .*
> *. . . He and I, my relatives,*
> *And my children, stay in this land,*
> *Drenched in sea spray.*
> *Where fish are caught in the hands.*
> *Waipi'o is drowsy in the mist.*
> - traditional Waipi'o song (Elbert and Mahoe 1970, 94)

WAIPI'O (CURVING Waters) Valley is a beautiful place, blessed with misty mountains, two magnificent waterfalls, a clear stream, lush, green taro fields, and a black-sand beach. It was the abode of the legendary king Wākea, ancestor of all Hawaiians, and Milu, ruler of the underworld. Later, the powerful king 'Umi and his sons

Līloa and Hākau lived their lives of drama and intrigue here. The valley has been inhabited for over one thousand years. At one time thousands of Hawaiians lived and farmed here, and even *menehune*, small legendary people, were reported to have lived here.

The valley was often chosen as a meeting place for the chiefs when important decisions, such as the succession of rulers, had to be made. The cliffs contain the secret burial caves of many powerful chiefs, and the spiritual power contained in their bones is said to remain in the valley. But life was not all work. Legends say that the gods Kāne and Kanaloa drank large amounts of their favorite *'awa* here.

The remains of six large *heiau* are spread throughout the valley, some of which are *luakini heiau*. At one huge event, eighty victims were offered in sacrifice and Kū was said to have come down from the heavens in a black cloud and a rainbow to lick up the human offerings with a tongue of fire.

The remains of Pāka'alana Pu'uhonua, a place of refuge for *kapu* breakers, stand in a grove of trees on the right-hand side of the beach, as you face the sea. It was built in the twelfth century, and its huge walls were hit by the tsunami of 1946. Residents said that the sound of the rocks falling as the huge wave demolished them exploded through the valley. Remains of Honua'ula Heiau are nearby. A tunnel is said to have connected the two temples.

A shark-man lived in a pool connected to the sea by a lava tunnel. Appearing as a man, he would warn residents about sharks as they passed his pool on the way to fish. Frequent shark attacks and his constant warnings aroused the suspicions of the residents, who ripped the clothing from his back and discovered a huge shark mouth. The shark-man dove into his pool and escaped to Maui waters.

A supernatural spirit appears as a yellow dog, sometimes small and sometimes huge. He came to Waipi'o to steal a conch shell that was being used to summon spirits. The shell was inherited by Kamehameha the Great and is now in the Bishop Museum. Another dog-spirit lives in the rock walls on the road down to the valley and comes to warn of danger.

Night marchers are seen in the valley, drums and nose flutes are heard, and sometimes torches flicker in the night. Waipi'o Valley is a leaping place of the soul. There is a "door to the dead" at the black-sand beach, where the soul enters the dark

Waipi'o Valley Cliffs

unknown of eternity, a region of twilight and shades, the netherworld of spirits who have not heeded the advice of their *'aumakua*. Here, the famished ghosts of men flee each other's presence in fear and suspicion.

The newly born Kamehameha I was hidden here and escaped the jealous king and warriors who sought to kill him. Because of his lonely upbringing in the valley, the little boy was called Kamehameha, "the lonely one." When he was a young man, the war god, Kū, was presented to him in Waipi'o.

In 1791, Kamehameha's armies fought a great battle offshore of Waipi'o, "The Battle of the Red-Mouthed Gun," against the ruling chiefs of Maui, O'ahu, and Kaua'i. The muskets, swivel guns, and four-pound cannon on board Kamehameha's (captured) schooner, *Fair American*, manned by Isaac Davis and John Young (both also captured), were too much for the raiding warriors who retreated to Maui. This use of artillery gave Kamehameha the edge he needed to conquer and then unite the islands.
(References: Kamakau 1992, 162; Malo 1996, 114; Sterling 1978, 92; Stokes 1991, 159-63.)

The road down into Waipi'o Valley is nearly perpendicular, and the sight of two overturned vehicles abandoned at the bottom is daunting. Our driver, Mareko Richmond, however, inspired confidence. For one thing, he looked like a hero in an Indiana Jones movie, and he was also very, very nice.

We forded four rivers and simply drove down another before arriving at The Tree House, our accommodation for the night, twenty-five feet up a gigantic monkeypod tree. We had our own private one-thousand-foot Pāpala Waterfall, which crashed into four pools as it descended.

Linda Beech, the lovely owner of The Tree House, has been living in Waipi'o Valley for thirty years. When she first arrived, she camped in

18. Waipi'o Valley

a tent under the monkeypod tree. For three nights in a row she heard singing and chanting from the Pāpala Waterfall area. She tried to locate the source of the chanting, but as she got closer, it grew fainter. She finally realized that the sounds were not of this dimension. Linda, who holds a doctorate in psychology, believes that after seven hundred years of human sacrifice in the valley, many of the rituals are locked in time, and our senses sometimes pick up on their resonance.

Recently, a houseguest asked Linda, "Who are the people that chant at the waterfall?" The guest said she had even distinguished a chant as one venerating Kū. Mareko has also heard the chanting and says that drums are often heard on the nights of Kū.

Linda has seen an *akua lele* (fireball) darting through the trees at eye level at night, and one of her neighbors reportedly chased one for half a mile.

On another occasion two students staying in the vicinity came crashing through the jungle to Linda's house. They had seen a red glow surrounding her cottage and thought it was on fire. As they approached the glow, it vanished, and they saw the shapes of night marchers-chiefs and warriors wearing feathered helmets and cloaks.

I was hoping to hear the warriors chanting as we snuggled into our tree house bed. In the middle of the night Will gave a loud shout. This was fairly encouraging, if rather alarming. Half asleep, he said he'd heard

Waterfall deep in Waipi'o Valley

Island of Hawai'i

a voice speaking right into his ear. Then he suddenly leaped out of bed, gathered his camera and tripod, and went out fearlessly into the jungle to photograph the golden full moon shining over the waterfall. I wondered if he had been summonsed by night marchers, or something equally interesting, but he soon returned, somewhat mosquito-bitten, but safe! (The Tree House, tel. (808) 775-7160)

Directions: Proceed forty-nine miles north from Hilo on Highway 19, turn right, and head out of Honoka'a to the end of Highway 240. The view from the Waipi'o Valley Lookout is stunning. The road to the valley is very steep, and only accessible to four-wheel-drive vehicles. It is possible to telephone at the lookout for four-wheel-drive taxi service. It's easy to walk down the steep road into the valley; the road is less than a mile long, but remember you may have to walk back up again! (Waipi'o Valley Shuttle, tel. (808) 775-7121)

At left: Mareko Richmond, guide, at The Treehouse, above: author in The Treehouse, Waipi'o Valley.

18. Waipi'o Valley

Great Day Trips and Places to Stay on the Island of Hawai'i

Drive 1. Starting from Kailua-Kona or the Kohala Coast, visit: Mo'okini Heiau (Site 1), Kamehameha I Birthplace (Site 2), Lapakahi State Park (Site 3), Pu'ukoholā Heiau (Site 4), and petroglyphs at Puakō (Site 5).

Try to reach the petroglyph fields in the cool of the day, and explore the beautiful walking paths of the Mauna Lani Bay Hotel and Bungalows.

Great Place to Stay: The Mauna Lani Bay Hotel and Bungalows is a beautiful oasis in a field of black lava. The Mauna Lani treasures its surroundings and is proud of its heritage of Hawaiian hospitality. The hotel pamphlet "View into the Past" relates the history of the area and has a map of trails and ancient sites, including the Puakō petroglyph fields. The resort has tennis courts, swimming pools, a lagoon, and a beautiful beach. The sculptured golf course was carved out of lava rock. View the painted sunset from the Bay Terrace Restaurant (moderate) and after dinner, follow the perfect coastal walking trail past the tranquil fishponds. For more information contact the Mauna Lani Bay Hotel and Bungalows at (800) 367-2323 or (808) 885-6622. (Rates: expensive)

Drive 2. From Kailua-Kona, explore Ahu'ena Heiau (Site 7), Ku'emanu Heiau (Site 8), Keauhou Archaeological Complex (Site 9), Hikiau Heiau (Site 10), and Pu'uhonua o Hōnaunau (Site 11).

Snorkel at Kahalu'u Beach Park and have lunch on the terrace at Jameson's (inexpensive).

Great Places to Stay: King Kamehameha Kona Beach Hotel is a conveniently situated place from which to explore the night life of the pretty town of Kailua-Kona and cruise the restaurants and shops. It also has the only swimming beach in the area. This section of the coast was favored by royalty, and Kamehameha's Ahu'ena Heiau, on the grounds of the hotel, occupies a pristine position on the bay. For more information contact the King Kamehameha Kona Beach Hotel at (800) 367-2111 or (808) 329-2911. (Rates: moderate)

Island of Hawai'i

Farther down the coast is the attractive Outrigger Keauhou Beach Resort, which is built on a historic site that includes *heiau*, a fishpond with a mythical dragon lizard, and the reconstructed summer cottage of King Kamehameha III. For more information contact the Outrigger Keauhou Beach Resort at (800) 688-7444 or (808) 322-3441. (Rates: moderate)

Drive 3. You can't visit the Big Island without visiting Madame Pele at Kīlauea Volcano (Site 13). Drive the Crater Rim and the Chain of Craters Road, and try one of the fascinating hikes.

Great Place to Stay: A visit to the volcano is best if you stay over-night so that you can, hopefully, see the fiery red lava make its way to the shore. The solid stone and timber Kīlauea Lodge, set in the cool, lush forests of Volcano Village, welcomes you with a chorus of birdsong, a roaring fire, excellent dining under a vaulted open-beamed *koa* ceiling, and beautifully furnished bedrooms. For more information contact Kīlauea Lodge at (808) 967-7366. Special Hawaiian resident rates are available during the month of September. (Rates: moderate)

Drive 4. Kaʻū District: South Point and Kalalea Heiau (Site 12). Spend a morning exploring the lava tubes at Kula Kai Caverns, visit the *heiau* and scenic coastline at South Point, then visit Punaluʻu Black Sand Beach, where turtle watching is popular.

Drive 5. While in Hilo, visit the *Naha* Stone (Site 15) and Coconut Island (Site 16).

Great Place to Stay: The Hilo Hawaiian Hotel on Banyan Drive. This elegant hotel is set on beautiful grounds that overlook Hilo Bay and Coconut Island. For more information contact the Hilo Hawaiian Hotel at (800) 272-5275 or (808) 935-9361. (Rates: moderate)

Drive 6. The roller-coaster Saddle Road to Mauna Kea Volcano and observatories (Site 17).

Drive 7. The ravishingly beautiful drive up the coast to Waipiʻo Valley (Site 18). En route visit ʻAkaka Falls for an easy hike showing nature at her best. Nearby Kolekole Beach Park is a great place to picnic.

Great Place to Stay: The Tree House is a completely unique, memorable experience, and the first time we've ever slept twenty-five feet up a huge monkeypod tree with a private waterfall. This obliging waterfall even supplies a flushing toilet, right up the tree; you have to see it to believe it! Bring your own water and food. For more information on a Tarzan and Jane experience contact The Tree House at (808) 775-7160 or, if this line is not working, Waipi'o Valley Wagon Tours at (808) 775-9518 will take a message. (Rates: moderate)

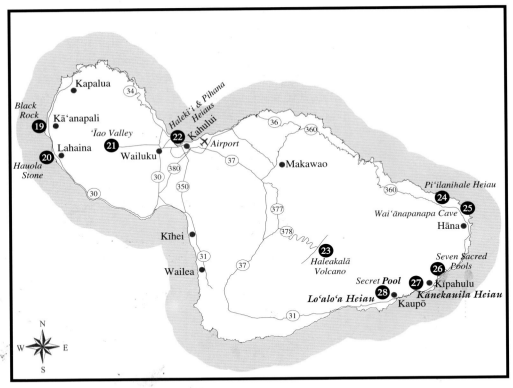

19. Puʻu Kekaʻa (Black Rock), Kāʻanapali-
Leaping place of the soul

> *A chief is a chief because of his subjects.*
> -Hawaiian saying

Puʻu Kekaʻa, an eighty-five-foot-high volcanic cinder cone, was a sacred place-a *leina a ka ʻuhane,* or leaping place of the soul. When a person lay dying, his soul would leave his body and wander about. If all earthly obligations had been fulfilled, the soul went to Puʻu Kekaʻa and left the island for the hereafter.

This area, at the attractive beach fronting the Sheraton Maui Resort, was once the site of a sacred *heiau* and old burial grounds. Many bloody battles were fought here, and a great many human bones and skeletons have been found. The historian Fornander stated that bones covered the sand during 1859-72. Anatomy students from Lahainaluna School in Maui came here for skeletons. .

Perfect swan dive at
Black Rock, leaping place of souls
(photo credit: Sheraton Maui)

Fornander related that many people died on this hill without apparent cause. Stones rolled down on travelers for no apparent reason. People said that this was a strange thing for a hill to do and declared, "Keka'a is ghostly! Keka'a is ghostly!"

The mighty Kahekili, Maui's last chief, enjoyed leaping dramatically from these rocks. Kahekili claimed the god of thunder as his ancestor. This god had initially been a man, Hekili, who lived in Pāpa'a'ea where thunder claps loudly and lightning strikes the forest. Hekili was known to have immense *mana*, because thunder and lightning destroyed his enemies. If people even whispered about him, thunder boomed, so his enemies ceased plotting against him.

When Hekili died, his body was cut into small pieces. People who had a piece had the *kuleana* (right) to worship thunder. When the god appeared, his right side was black from head to foot. Lightning wagged like a tongue licking at the bushes; smoke rose and offerings vanished into the air.

Kahekili, who claimed this prestigious ancestor, led a company of fierce warriors. He and the warriors were all tattooed blue-black from hairline to toe with elaborate designs on the right sides of their faces and bodies.

M a u i

Kahekili excelled at the popular sport of *lele kawa*, leaping feet first from high cliffs into the sea. His leaps from the cliff at Pu'u Keka'a (see also Site 30) were considered particularly brave because Pu'u Keka'a was a *kapu* and sacred place for souls to leap into the hereafter. It was believed that only a person of great spiritual strength could do this and survive. When his warriors noted his bravery, they were encouraged to follow him into battle.

At dusk an employee of the Sheraton Maui Resort now reenacts the famous eighteenth century leap of Kahekili. The dive into the sea is the dramatic highlight to the nightly torch-lighting ceremonies.

(References: Pukui, Haertig, and Lee 1972, 1: 152; Sterling 1998, 45-48.)

Willy, who braids ti leaves into great hats at the Lahaina wharf, used to cook at the Ritz-Carlton Hotel at Kapalua. Many of these resorts along the coast are built on what was considered sacred ground by the Hawaiians. Landscaped gardens and tennis courts cover heiau and burial grounds. Where are the spirits of the warriors now? Willy says he saw them on the walls one night as he vacuumed the long passages of the hotel. He was all by himself, but the walls were covered with shadowy figures.

Directions: Pu'u Keka'a is located at the Sheraton Maui Resort, 2605 Kā'anapali Parkway, Kā'anapali. Follow Kā'anapali Parkway to its end. Parking in the Sheraton Maui Resort lot costs two dollars per twenty minutes. Whaler's Village has parking for two dollars an hour, and the first three hours are free with validation. There is a nice beach in front of the Sheraton with great snorkeling among the fish and coral.

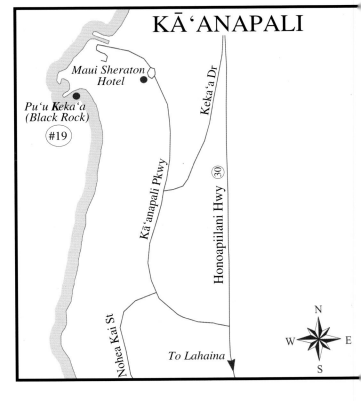

19. Pu'u Keka'a

Hauola Healing Stone with seat, angular back, and even a footrest

20. Hauola Stone, Lahaina-
Place of healing

> *To thee is this board [or other object] that injured*
> *The foot of [name]*
> *Return the flesh to the flesh, the blood to the blood,*
> *The vein to itself.*
> *Take away all pain.*
> *Benumb the numbness, the hit, remove every pain.*
> *Grant recovery.*
> *It is for thee, O Deity, to restore him.*
> *'āmama. It is free of tabu.*
> -Hawaiian prayer (Gutmanis 1983, 35)

This large stone resembles a spacious seat with a small angular back. At the foot of the stone is a hollow, perhaps worn from the many feet that have rested here. The stone stands in a cluster of large rocks that rise above the waves off the northern end of a stone wall fronting the public library grounds. *Kāhuna* sent patients here to sit on the stone and dangle their feet in the healing water. It is believed to have been one of the most powerful healing places in all of Hawai'i, and legend says that many were cured here.

Stones were very important to the ancient Hawaiians. Healing stones were found in areas holding powerful forces of nature that stilled the spirit and healed the soul. *Kāhuna* used herbs and plants, diet, massage, and healing stones for their patients.

This sacred stone was also used as a *pōhaku piko*. It was important to hide the *piko* completely; if a rat took it, the child would become a disgrace to his parents. "*Piko* taken by the rats" was an effective insult, and parents would often give away a child whose *piko* was taken by rats.

Legend says that the stone is a young girl, Hauola, who was turned to stone by the gods to protect her from her enemies.

Another distraught young girl who once walked along this oceanfront was the little Princess Nahi'ena'ena. As the sacred daughter of Kamehameha the Great and Keōpūolani, his sacred wife, it was customary that she marry her sacred brother, a *naha* union blessed by the gods. This union protected the royal *mana*. She was happy about that as she loved her brother, the young Kamehameha III, dearly.

Tragically, the clash of two worlds destroyed Nahi'ena'ena. The missionaries were horrified when they learned about the intended marriage, for in their world it was incest. Nahi'ena'ena was fond of her missionary teachers and found herself torn between her hope of pleasing them and her wish to marry her brother.

The confused young king, Kamehameha III, became a teenage alcoholic who was too high in rank to be controlled by anyone. He declared that he alone was the ultimate law, and he and the princess lived together, defying the missionaries. Eventually Nahi'ena'ena was persuaded by the missionaries to marry another chief from the Big Island, but she continued to sleep with her brother and soon fell pregnant. The child and the twenty-one-year-old princess both died, and her people grieved for her. They considered her a sacrificial victim and named the street of her funeral procession *Luakini* (Sacrifice) Street.

(References: Gutmanis 1977; Kamakau 1992, 339, 340; Sterling 1998, 34.)

There are a large number of healers on Maui, including doctors of oriental medicine, Shakti practitioners, rebirthing specialists, hypnotists, iridologists, psychics, and many more. Is this because Maui is an energy center, blessed with a large share of the earth's energy force?

We searched for more information on Hawaiian healers and visited Maui Noni, where Herbert and Lona Moniz produce capsules of the amazing noni plant. Lona told us that the precious noni had been

20. *Hauola Stone*

brought to Hawai'i by early Polynesian settlers who packed the young shoots carefully into canoes between bananas, taro, and yams for long ocean voyages. Lona makes no claims that noni can cure a disease, but clients report experiencing noticeable and remarkable results in their various conditions. Former University of Hawaii researcher R. M. Heinicke states that the natural xeronine in noni may help high blood pressure, senility, menstrual cramps, arthritis, gastric ulcers, sprains, mental depression, arteriosclerosis, drug addiction, and pain. Patients with diabetes and lupus have reported improvement, and noni is especially effective on diabetic ulcers. We were really convinced- noni seems to offer a veritable pharmacy! For more information call Maui Noni at (808) 878-1861.

Directions: The healing stone is in the shallow water fronting the public library grounds at the northern end of Wharf Street, adjacent to the *Carthaginian*, a replica of the nineteenth-century fast freighter that brought the first commerce to the Hawaiian Islands. Luakini Street is nearby and is listed as one of the sites in the Lahaina Historic Walking Tour.

Lahaina was once a bustling seaport humming with eager whalers, nubile maidens, and zealous missionaries. It is an attractive town and fun to explore. When you need a break you can enjoy a cocktail on the veranda of the Pioneer Inn-Errol Flynn did. For a map of the thirty-one sites featured in the self-guided Lahaina Historic Walking Tour, ask at the Baldwin home on the corner of Dickenson and Front Street, or at the conveniently located Maui Islander Hotel, 660 Wainee Street. The Lahaina map in *This Week* magazine marks the sites.

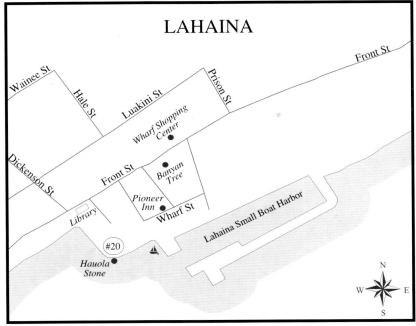

'Īao Needle dominates 'Īao Valley

21. 'Īao Valley, Wailuku-
Phallic rock of the god Kanaloa

'Io dwelt within the breathing space of immensity,
The universe was in darkness, with water everywhere,
There was no glimmer of dawn, no clearness, no light.
And he began by saying these words,
That he might cease remaining inactive,
Darkness, become a light-possessing darkness!
And at once light appeared.
-Polynesian chant (Handy et al. 1965, 49)

THE 2,250-FOOT-HIGH 'Īao Needle, the amazing phallic rock of the god Kanaloa, dominates this lush green valley. In prehistoric ages, ancient Hawaiians named this valley 'Īao (Supreme Light), in honor of the one supreme creator god 'Io, and people made pilgrimages from far points of the island to pay homage. The valley is filled with *mana* from its highest peak, Pu'u Kukui, to the shoreline of Kahului Bay.

This was the heart of the ancient kingdom of Maui and a favorite place of the *ali'i*. As it was one of the most important political centers, many battles took place here, and hundreds of warriors died. The valley has an eerie sense of history. There are stories of ghosts drifting below the massive cliffs.

The bones of many ancient kings are hidden in a secret cave to protect their *mana* from misuse. The last Hawaiian king, King Kalākaua, made extensive investigations to try to locate the cave but was unsuccessful.

In the fifteenth century Maui was ruled by King Kaka'e, a king so sacred that even taking a peep at him or allowing his shadow to fall upon you was punishable by death. King Kaka'e was a kind ruler who loved his people. Rather than risk having to condemn anyone to death, he lived like a hermit in a cave in a *kapu* part of the valley. This area is called Ka Pili o Kaka'e (Companion of Kaka'e), in reference to a huge stone that stood before the cave. The king hid from his people behind the stone, so the people respected the stone because of the thoughtfulness of their monarch.
(Reference: Sterling 1998, 79-80, 100.)

When the County of Maui was bulldozing the present parking area, a Hawaiian bulldozer operator came across King Kaka'e's stone. He was unable to move it and realized that it had mana. The Hawaiians of 'Iao Valley told him that it had been King Kaka'e's companion. The bulldozer operator prayed and asked the guardian spirit of the stone to allow it to move to safety, explaining that if it didn't go it would be dynamited. The stone then allowed itself to be easily moved into the middle of Kapela Stream. A flash flood arose that washed down the stream and hid the stone.
(Reference: Honolulu Star-Bulletin, 24 July 1960, Hawaiian Life section.)

Directions: Travel four miles west of Wailuku to the end of 'Iao Valley Road (Highway 320). The area has beautiful walking trails and wheelchair access. The cave, which is across the stream from the coach parking area, is largely blocked from view by bushes, and a steep embankment makes attempted viewing somewhat risky.

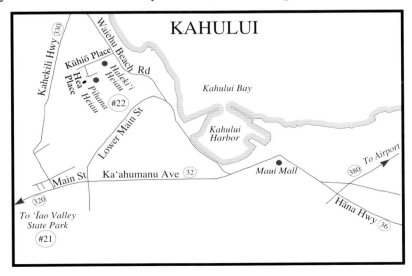

22. Haleki'i and Pihana Heiau, Kahului-
Temple of high supernatural beings

> *Silent and attentive are the rude and unceremonious,*
> *Silent are the wicked and the unbelievers,*
> *Silent are the hula dancers,*
> *Silent are those given to sports and games,*
> *Silent are the hot-blooded ones,*
> *Give us now the blood of swine!*
> *Give us now the blood of dogs!*
> *The blood of the human sacrifice!*
> *The deity is silent.*
> -Hawaiian chant (Gutmanis 1983, 40)

THESE *HEIAU* are among Maui's most interesting historical sights. They are so old that it is believed that the *menehune* built the original structures. The *heiau* are of a considerable size, and their position on a high sand dune makes them extremely impressive.

These massive temples were built from large, smooth, waterworn rocks hauled up to the ridge from ʻĪao Stream. The terraces are paved with *ʻiliʻili* stones brought up in baskets. The incredible amount of work that went into the building of these *heiau* attests to the power of the chiefs to command their people. The size of the *heiau* attests to the significance of the Wailuku region as a religious site.

The *heiau* closest to the parking lot is Halekiʻi (House of Images). Carved images of the gods were set up on the platforms to keep enemies away. The images, with their big heads and scowling mouths, were ferocious-looking and intended to inspire fear. Often their tongues stuck out, a common Polynesian gesture of defiance in war dances. The staring eyes were a symbol of spirit force and power. The statues themselves were not gods, but shrines that the gods could be induced to enter on occasion. Two image posts were dug up in a field near the *heiau*. One was eight feet tall, with the head occupying over half the length of the image. It had a wide open mouth, slanting eyes, and the suggestion of horns. The ten-foot-high image was a succession of heads.

This was a *heiau* for ceremonies honoring family gods. The several house sites were those of chiefs and royal families, and the entire sand dune was probably reserved for *aliʻi*. The most sacred high chiefess, Keōpūolani, was born here in 1780. She became Kamehameha the Great's sacred wife. Because of her high birth, the young girl was so sacred that Kamehameha had to enter her dwelling naked and on his knees. Their children were also sacred, and it was *kapu* for Kamehameha to stand in their presence. He would lie down and have little Prince Liholiho sit on his chest.

Keōpūolani's parents were sister and half-brother, a *naha* union. Her father's ancestors had ruled Hawaiʻi for as many generations back as genealogies extend. Thus, her genealogy traced back to the gods, and Keōpūolani's *kapu* was equal to that of the gods. When she was a baby, only her wet nurse could touch her. Neither chief nor commoner dared approach or touch her; anyone who broke this *kapu* would be put to death. Everyone in her presence had to prostrate himself. She was gentle and considerate and never walked out during daylight hours, as it would mean certain death to anyone who stepped in her shadow.

Pihana-a-ka-lani (gathering place of high supernatural beings) was a sacrificial temple where human sacrifices were made to ensure success in war and crops. The powerful tattooed high chief Kahekili worshiped here. When Maui was conquered, rebellious high chiefs were sacrificed here, but only if their lineage was untainted.

Tradition relates that the last sacrifice here was a young girl, Poloahilani, the half-sister of a Maui high chiefess. It was unusual for women to be sacrificed, but the high chiefess had insulted the mighty conquerors and was chosen to be sacrificed to the war god, Kū. Poloahilani, who was not of such high royal blood, came in her place on the advice of the Maui priests. The high chiefess lived the rest of her life incognito.

Today, groups of Nakoa warriors, who practice the ancient Hawaiian martial art of Lua and seek to acquire *mana*, make offerings here.

(References: Kamakau 1992, 149, 188, 244, 261; Sterling 1998, 72, 75-78.)

Two groups are actively involved with the heiau today. We spoke to Jacob Mau, a fine-looking Hawaiian kupuna, who blessed us with his spirit of aloha. He told us about Lua, the ancient Hawaiian martial art practiced by Nakoa (The Strong) warriors. Young men trained as Nakoa had to be powerful physically and mentally. They had to control their minds, tempers, and emotions. The Hawaiian ali'i and warriors were all trained in these skills. Physically, the Nakoa warriors had incredible fighting abilities.

The art of Lua was supposed to be used for good purposes, but if it was taken to extremes, Lua training included learning how to pierce a man's chest and tear out his heart. Lua warriors could pull a man's intestines through his rectum.

Some men are practicing Lua in secret today. In their quest for mana, some Nakoa are going to the luakini heiau and calling on the warrior spirits and gods. They say the spirits of the ancient warriors have answered the calls. However, a relative of the Pi'ilani family in Hāna warned, "If you call them, they will eat you."

Daniel Kikawa, author of the book Perpetuated in Righteousness, told us about Ka Po'e o 'Io (The People of God). Jacob Mau is a member of this group of men and women, who after a year's planning and re- search, formed an organization to ask forgiveness from God for the human sacrifice that occurred at the luakini heiau and to seek cleansing of the land (See Site 24-Pi'ilanihale Heiau). Many of these spiritual warriors are Hawaiian, and some are descendants of the ali'i who ruled

22. Haleki'i and Pihana Heiau

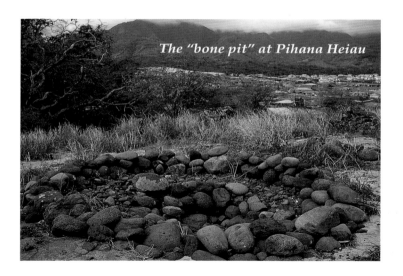

The "bone pit" at Pihana Heiau

the districts. They also have ancestors who were among the common people oppressed by the harsh system of kapu laws.

For more information, write to 'Io Project, Aloha Ke Akua Ministries, HCR2 Box 6640, Kea'au, Hawaii 96749.

Directions: From the Kahului airport take Highway 340 to Wai'ehu, then take Wai'ehu Beach Road over a bridge. Turn left at Kūhiō Place and then left again on Hea Place, where a sign points the way to the state monument.

(See map page 69)

Kamoali'i cinder cone
(photo courtesy of National Parks Service)

23. Haleakalā Volcano, Makawao- *Strongest natural power point in the United States*

Haleakalā (HOUSE of the Sun) is the largest dormant volcano in the world, so high at 10,023 feet that mists surround the summit and clouds float below it. Haleakalā is truly majestic. The U.S. Air Force has a high-tech facility with satellite tracking stations here dubbed "Science City," and their research indicates Haleakalā is the strongest natural power point in America. There is an energy configuration coming from the earth and a high focus of radiation coming from outside the atmosphere. The volcano sits like a mighty pyramid in the Pacific. According to Mike Townsend, park ranger and naturalist, the huge, iron-rich cinder cone called Magnetic Peak has a magnetic field strong enough to deflect a compass needle.

The crater of the volcano is an awesome sight. The cinder cones within are volcanic vents that may form electromagnetic lines from the center of the earth. Students of higher consciousness from around the world are attracted to the energy force here and believe it accelerates personal growth. This is a true place of power.

How does this concentration of energy affect the surrounding areas? We drove to Makawao, a small town on the slopes of the crater, to ask for more details. Makawao is a colorful cowboy town where the half-century old, one-story buildings are crammed with unique stores and restaurants. The town is absolutely full of healers. There are billboards and pamphlets offering spiritual healing and counseling from practitioners of holistic healing, Chinese herbal medicine, craniosacral therapy, massage therapy, iridology, psychic consulting, rebirthing, ascension acceleration, holistic beauty, feng shui, horse-whispering therapy, shamanic journeys, and many, many more. Arriving there was rather like climbing out of the car into a coven of friendly witches. Is this the reason most people walking on the street and in the stores are clear-skinned with wide-open, shining eyes and blissful smiles?

We went to the Dragon's Den, a store full of little bottles of herbal remedies, crystals, beads, and books, and asked if the high energy at the crater was the reason for the large number of healers in the area. This was the right place to go. Matthew, one of the amazingly good-looking residents, nodded vigorously, and his pretty young companion shook her shining ringlets in agreement-of course it was! Matthew told us one could be helped by a healer to benefit from the energy, but basically it was a personal journey. The forces at the crater were both light and dark and not always used for good. A powerful place like this on the earth's magnetic grid can also used to send out forces of evil, hatred, and fear.

Early Hawaiians considered Haleakalā to be sacred and also considered the vortex to be one of the strongest natural power points on Earth. Ancient Hawaiians did not live here as it was too cool and barren. They used the crater for spiritual ceremonies and crossed it on foot. Remains of the ancient Pi'ilani Highway still exist within the crater. Several *heiau* were built here, including the very sacred one at Mt. Haleakalā, an 8,200-foot-high peak along the south, near the Kaupō Gap. Tradition says that *kāhuna* were initiated at this *heiau*. Platforms and sleeping shelters, possibly from these *kāhuna* schools, can be found among the rocks. Power struggles took place at the top of the volcano between the healing practitioners, the *kāhuna lapaʻau*, and their rivals, the *kāhuna ʻanāʻanā*, the black-magic sorcerers.

The *aliʻi* were buried in secret caves, and the bodies of commoners were thrown into a bottomless pit to protect the bodies from sorcery. Altars, cairns, and shrines were built here. Many are now gone, covered by the shifting cinders. These sands were considered so sacred that even scratching them could mean death. Three people discovered this when, according to the legend, they scratched the sands and were buried by cinders.

Many legends are associated with Haleakalā. It was once the home of the fiery goddess Pele, before she moved to Kīlauea. The demigod Maui snared the sun here, so his mother would have longer to sun-dry her *kapa* cloth. Pele's fearsome shark-god brother lived in the crater, and even powerful Pele dared not allow the smoke from her fires to trespass on the terrible sanctity of her brother's abode. He roams the deep waters of Maui in his shark form, and some Hawaiians claim him as their spiritual guide or *ʻaumakua*.
(References: Pukui, Elbert, and Mookini 1989, 36; Sterling 1998, 260-67.)

Night marchers carry out their mysterious activities near their burial caves on the Kaupō lava fields at the base of the volcano.

Jacob Mau, whose ancestors were the original owners of part of the Kaupō land, and who grew up in this area, told us of his relative's encounter with the night marchers.

The young man had gone hunting goats on the land. He was riding home with the dead goats tied to the rump of his horse when he heard drums and flutes. Looking over the lava fields, he saw the night marchers walking above the ground and proceeding in his direction.

He'd heard the correct way to handle night marchers was to take off your clothing, prostrate yourself before them, and hope for the best, but as he was frantically deciding what to do, his horse took off and galloped down the trail, jumping the two gates. He lost all his goats.

Directions: Take Highway 37 from Kahului, then turn left onto Highway 377, above Pukalani, and turn left again onto Highway 378 for the last ten winding miles. The Sun Visitor Center is located on the crater rim. It is the highest point on Maui, and the glassed-in vantage point is good for sunrise viewing. A two-and-a-half-hour hike down Sliding Sands Trail into the crater is offered every Saturday, Sunday, and

Iron rich Magnetic Peak with Mauna Kea and Mauna Loa behind

Tuesday at 10 a.m.; meet at the visitor center. There are thirty miles of well-marked trails. Cabins can be rented, but apply early, preferably ninety days in advance. Write to the Superintendent, Haleakalā National Park, Box 369, Makawao, Maui 96768. The bike ride down Haleakalā is exhilarating for the fearless.

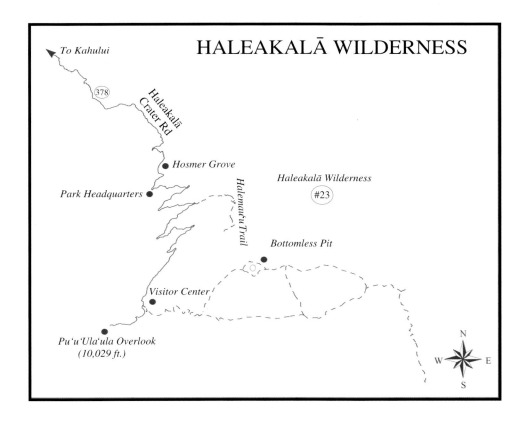

HALEAKALĀ WILDERNESS

To Kahului
378
Haleakalā Crater Rd
Hosmer Grove
Park Headquarters
Halemau'u Trail
Haleakalā Wilderness
#23
Bottomless Pit
Visitor Center
Pu'u'Ula'ula Overlook
(10,029 ft.)

Maui

Immense tiered and terraced Pi'ilanihale Heiau

24. Pi'ilanihale Heiau, Hāna-
Largest sacrificial heiau in Hawai'i

Behold the gods
Of Havai'i, the birthplace of lands,
Of Havai'i, the birthplace of gods,
Of Havai'i, the birthplace of people!
Gods inside, gods outside,
Gods above, gods below,
Gods oceanward, gods landward,
Gods incarnate, gods not incarnate,
Gods punishing sins, gods pardoning sins,
Gods devouring men, gods slaying warriors,
Gods saving men,
Gods of darkness, gods of light,
Gods of the ten skies.
Can the gods be counted?
The gods cannot all be counted!
-Polynesian chant (Luomala 1986, 63)

Brooding Pi'ilanihale Heiau, standing on the wildly beautiful cliffs of Honomā'ele, is the largest *heiau* in the Hawaiian Islands-with massive, 50-foot-high walls and estimated dimensions of 340 by 415 feet, it is bigger than a football field.

The original *heiau* was built in the thirteenth century and was extended by the High Chief Pi'ilani, who came from the western side of Maui in 1570 and conquered the chiefs of the fertile Hāna region. The temple was probably consecrated with human sacrifices (Sterling 1998, 11), but it might not have been a *luakini heiau* in its last phase of use, according to the archaeologists involved in the restoration, who found artifacts suggesting residential use.

The five-tiered, terraced platforms, positioned on a ridge of lava rock, tower overhead. There are two separate platforms, connected by a large central terrace, a forty-foot-deep stone-filled gully, and an eight-foot-high stone wall. The *heiau* commands a breathtaking view of the surrounding coastline.

This was the heart of an ancient kingdom, the royal abode of the great Pi'ilani family of Maui chiefs, who flourished in the sixteenth century. Archaeologists estimate that 84,000 person-days of labor went into the construction of the early *heiau*, and 43,000 person-days were required for the modifications. Imagine the *ali'i*, clad in their capes and helmets of red and yellow feathers, walking on these huge platforms, directing their subjects, and gazing in pride at their fertile lands.

Why is a *heiau* of this incredible size shrouded in mystery and not referred to in any Hawaiian chant? Chipper Wichman, the Director of Kahanu Garden, told us that one possible reason is that talking about the *heiau* was made *kapu* by Kiha-a-Pi'ilani.

When the benevolent High Chief Pi'ilani died, there were two heirs to the kingdom, his sons Lono-a-Pi'ilani and Kiha-a-Pi'ilani. They quarreled, and Lono sought to kill Kiha, who fled in secret to Moloka'i. Kiha, who was as militant as his brother, joined forces with the powerful king of Hawai'i, 'Umi-a-Līloa. He also found time to surf with and marry the beautiful Kōleamoku, who was betrothed to his brother.

'Umi agreed to help Kiha acquire the kingdom, and a year was spent building war canoes and preparing for war. When Kiha and 'Umi finally attacked Maui, their canoes were so great in number that the first ones reached Hāna while the last ones were still on Hawai'i.

50-foot high North West Wall of Pi'ilanihale Heiau towers over the author

For a while the warriors of Maui were successful. Leading their defense was Ho'olae, a small, fearless warrior known for his strong hands. The battle raged during the day, and at night the Maui warriors slept peacefully, as Ho'olae had mounted a large wooden image with a huge club above the tower on Ka'uiki Hill. The Hawai'i chiefs feared this large warrior and dared not approach while he stood guard. Eventually a brave Hawai'i warrior spotted the deception and dismantled the wooden figure. The Hawai'i warriors routed the Maui troops, and the strong hands of the brave Ho'olae were brought to Kiha as he had instructed. Lono, it was said, died in fear.

Kiha divided the Hāna lands and put a *kapu* on any talk of his brother, Lono. The massive Pi'ilanihale Heiau was made *kapu* and eventually stood in silence, covered in dank vines and twisting plants. Today descendants of the family say that they were forbidden, as children, to go to the *heiau*.
(References: Kamakau 1992, 22-31; Kirch 1996, 72; Kirch 1985, 144, 147; Sterling 1998, 11, 12, 123.)

"If you call them, they will eat you."

In March 1998, members of the smallest church in Hāna, Maui, visited the largest heiau, hoping that through prayer they could cleanse the land of past evils associated with human sacrifice.

According to the church report, as the men approached the heiau, seven women intercessors prayed at the bottom of the hill on which the heiau stood. The men hiked up the hill and the pastor saw a warrior standing on the wall confronting them. Suddenly, the warrior turned and fled, and chariots appeared in the sky. All seven of the women confirmed seeing the same vision. The pastor and his church were ready to struggle with demons to return the heiau to God, but felt the peace and love of God instead ('Io Project Report, Aloha Ke Akua Ministries).

We spoke to a relative of the Pi'ilani family, who related that people had been calling spirits at the heiau. They had suffered a terrible family tragedy and therefore requested that the heiau be prayed over. The relative was very reluctant to discuss calling the spirits of warriors and stated, "If you call them, they will eat you."

According to a tour guide of the gardens, the family had recently received a grant to restore the heiau. One of the conditions of the grant was admission of the public to the heiau, but the family was now most reluctant to allow the public anywhere near the heiau.

Directions: Near Hāna Airport, turn from Hāna Highway onto 'Ula'ino Road and proceed about 1.5 miles along a rough road to Kahanu Garden on your right. An HVB (Hawai'i Visitors Bureau) warrior sign

is at the gate. The *heiau* **is within the grounds of the lush Kahanu Garden, and access is only available during the usual visiting hours for the gardens. Guided tours of the gardens take place at 11 a.m. and 1 p.m. Monday through Friday, and have to be booked in advance- call (808) 248-8912.**

For an unexpected delight, after visiting the garden, continue down the winding 'Ula'ino Road to the parking area at the end. To the left of the beach, clamber a short distance over large boulders to Blue Pool, where an idyllic waterfall drops fresh water into a deep oceanside pool.

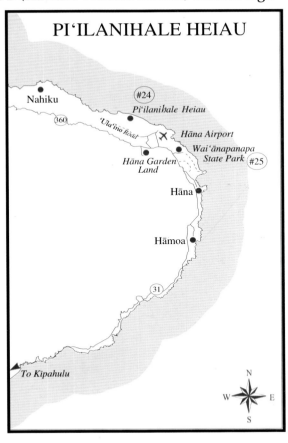

PI'ILANIHALE HEIAU

Nahiku
#24
Pi'ilanihale Heiau
360
'Ula'ino Road
Hāna Airport
Wai'ānapanapa State Park
#25
Hāna Garden Land
Hāna
Hāmoa
31
To Kīpahulu

N
W   E
S

25. Wai'ānapanapa Cave, Hāna-
Scene of ancient murder

THE ANCIENT King's Highway runs along the cliff at Wai'ānapanapa State Park, where wild seas crash onto surreal black beaches and waves roar through lava tubes and large natural arches. Ancient *heiau* blend with the weirdly-shaped rocks. The mountains are honeycombed with caves and caverns and lava tubes leading to the ocean.

The tunnel-like trail to Wai'ānapanapa (Water Flashing Rainbow) Cave runs through a twisting *hau* tree forest and is lined with orchids. The cave is named for the rainbow stones sent by the gods at the death of a young princess who, legend says, was murdered here.

The beautiful princess Pōpō'alaea escaped from her cruel and jealous husband and hid with her companion and maid, Mānona, in this cave by swimming underwater through a cold freshwater pool. The chief searched furiously for his young wife. He heard rumors that she had been seen at Wai'ānapanapa, so he came here with his warriors. Looking into the water of the cave, he saw the reflections of a feathered *kāhili* that Mānona was fanning back and forth.

He and his warriors jumped into the water, swam into the cave, and savagely murdered the two women. Their blood and even their brain particles are said to still stain the cave walls.

The waters of the cave turn red on the nights of Kū, when the night is darkest and the moon is a thin sickle moon. In the spring, when the tragedy took place, red shrimp make the stones turn an even redder hue. Tradition says this is either a sign of forgiveness or the casting out of an evil spirit.
(References: Beckwith 1970, 381; Sterling 1998, 125-26.)

As we stood staring intently into the large, dark cave, some adventurous Hawaiian teenagers, equipped with torches in plastic covers, dived into the clear water of the pool. They swam through a rock opening and disappeared into the adjoining hidden cave-probably where the princess and her maid once hid. Our daughter, Juliet, and son, Adam, plunged into the icy waters, following the teenagers. They swam under the ledge and surfaced in a strange, dark cave. The lichen on the cave walls looked like brain particles, and they wondered what was swimming in the water with them. They left hurriedly!

There is obviously a complex system of lava tube caves here. Aaron, our son-in-law, climbed into an entrance above the Wai'ānapanapa Cave and appeared some time later out of an opening on the top of the cliff. Interested in the mysterious lava tubes, we decided to go deep down into Hāna's underground, the nearby two-mile-long Ka'elekū Caverns lava tube. Chuck Thorne of Maui Cave Adventures led us into a magic world down there-glistening chocolate stalactites, cascading lava falls, "moon-milk" mineral deposits, large pillars, and rare grapelike cluster formations of lava. The tube was pitch dark until we reached Dancing Sunbeam skylight, which offered a window to the world above and fresh, cool air. The immense lava tube has forty-foot-high ceilings in places and seems to go on forever. Chuck is still exploring and recently discovered a new chamber, accessed through a narrow crawl space. Dedicated spelunkers can crawl through tunnels to dark-chocolate worlds of softly dripping water, pale, blind insects and skeletons of bats.

Hawaiians used the lava tubes as traveling passages for runners and for hiding women and children during the fierce battles of long ago.

Chuck Thorne offers two, four, and six-hour guided explorations daily. Phone Maui Cave Adventures at (808) 248-7308 or visit their web site at http://www.mauicave.com.

At Wai'ānapanapa State Park a three-mile-long stone trail along the coast follows part of the ancient King's Highway and leads to a small *heiau*. Drums are said to be heard from this *heiau* at night. The lush vegetation hides other ancient stone platforms and burial cairns.

Directions: Drive 52.8 miles east of Kahului Airport, on the very winding, very scenic Hāna Highway (Highway 360). Wai'ānapanapa State Park is about two to three miles before Hāna, after the airport turnoff. Watch for the sign and turn left. The *heiau* is about a half-mile along the King's Trail toward Hāna, near a dilapidated fence.
A blowhole that we passed on the King's Trail sounded ominously like warriors' drums. Highlights of the area include the remote and beautiful volcanic coastline, black-sand beaches, *heiau*, and caves. Camping sites and cabins are available.

(See map page 81)

Black sand beach and jagged rocks below the cave

25. Wai'ānapanapa Cave

'Ohe'o Gulch- Seven Sacred Pools

26. Beyond Hāna, 'Ohe'o Gulch-
Seven sacred pools

DARK, DEEP pools, cascading waterfalls and rapids, and the enchantment of the whispering, dark, green bamboo forests, give the Seven Sacred Pools of 'Ohe'o Gulch their own *mana*, and a sense of the Creator's presence.

The *kapu* pools were reserved for the *ali'i*, and each pool was guarded by two warriors. There are more than seven pools, but seven was a mystical number to the Hawaiians. The seven pools were known as Nā Wai Nāhiku, referring to one of the most noted constellations in the heavens, the Big Dipper, which was often used by Hawaiian navigators.

The pools are said to represent man's search for perfection, which is represented in the climb from the brackish sea pool up to the seventh and biggest pool, Nā Hiku, where you look up at the waterfall. When young people erred, their parents hoped to bring them back to perfection through this ascent. The full name of the gulch is 'Ohe'o-Kapo (bamboo of Kapo) referring to the goddess Kapo, a goddess of hula and fierce sorcery, and the bamboo represents her slender form as she sways.

(Reference: J. Medeiros, "A True Story of the Seven Sacred Pools of Kīpahulu," Maui News, 28 March 1964 and 14 August 1965.)

We started the hike to Waimoku Falls, winding up the sloping trail. The weather was strange; hot sunshine with the occasional bucket of chilling rain dumped from above. The blue lower pools of the Seven Sacred Pools were full of blissful people, but the higher ones remained unoccupied and serene. The only sound was of gushing water as it streamed over rocks and down gullies. We came to a meadow full of guava trees and sank into the tall, sweet-smelling grass. How many pink, juicy guavas can you eat before you get a stomach ache?

A high bridge crossed cascading Makahiku Falls and led into the dark thickets of a dense bamboo forest. It was wonderful here- bamboo rattled and creaked, and slivers of sunshine moved across the trail. A boardwalk provided an easy path over the mud and then suddenly came to an end. Was this where they separated the men from the boys? Did I want to get my hiking boots and socks saturated with mud? Was it worth it? Will sarcastically suggested that I write a travel adventure book called "Great Places I Never Actually Got To", which gave me incentive to keep going. Two small children, wearing rubber dive boots, came slipping and sliding by. I pressed on and yes, Waimoku Falls, descending in shimmering, misty sheets, was worth it.

Directions: From Hāna, follow Route 31 for ten miles. The parking area is next to the Ranger Station at Kīpahulu. For the hike to Waimoku Falls, cross the road, go back one hundred yards, and ascend the trail at the grassy knoll.

27. Kānekauila Heiau– *Temple for a lightning-wielding god and a secret pool*

Lei-bedecked cross on former Catholic Church foundation, with the altar of Kānekauila Heiau in the background

KĀNEKAUILA (LIGHTNING WIELDER) Heiau, a gloomy *heiau* measuring 220 by 210 feet, is positioned on a cliff directly across the ocean from the fearsome Moʻokini Heiau, no doubt providing excellent views of the flames from both altars. Eddie Pu, a *kupuna* and a ranger at Kīpahulu, told us this was primarily a navigational *heiau*, but it was also used for human sacrifices, as were most of the Kaupō *heiau*.

On the large platform, old Christian graves huddle together facing the *heiau* altar. Their former protector, a small church, has been relocated two hundred yards down the road, leaving only the incongruously placed graves and the church foundation, marked by a rusty, lei-bedecked cross. Why was it moved and under what circumstances? After many inquiries, we have not yet found the answers.

A secret pool: We drove down the winding Kaupō road, an experience similar to being in a real-life Nintendo game. Mostly we cowered behind a tourist bus for protection from the oncoming traffic. At small Alelele Bridge, we noticed three people making their way through the long grass on a narrow trail. We followed them and soon came to a magic circle of

Secret Pool and waterfall

stone terraces and round rocks. We wondered if this had been a healing *heiau*, as there were many noni trees, which are favored by Hawaiian healers. A large, altar-size rock held smooth lava stones wrapped in ti leaves and the recent remains of burnt *kukui* nut lamps. The *kukui* nuts which contain a flammable oil, can be used for torches and lighting and are associated with the calling of spirits.

The trail continued for five minutes to a hidden treasure-a magical waterfall and pristine natural pool.

Directions: From the ranger station at Kīpahulu, head toward Kaupō for less than a mile. Pass two aluminum gates on your left, and stop at a third with two tall palm trees and a low stone wall. Follow the shady path one minute to the *heiau* and graveyard.

To get to the secret pool, drive three miles from the ranger station, and just after a "Blow Horn" sign you will reach Alelele Bridge. Take the trail on the right just before the bridge and proceed inland about ten minutes.

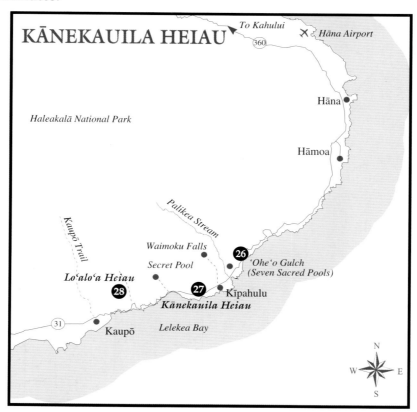

KĀNEKAUILA HEIAU

To Kahului
360
Hāna Airport
Haleakalā National Park
Hāna
Hāmoa
Palikea Stream
Kaupō Trail
Waimoku Falls
26
'Ohe'o Gulch (Seven Sacred Pools)
Secret Pool
Lo'alo'a Heiau
28
27
Kīpahulu
Kānekauila Heiau
31
Kaupō
Lelekea Bay

N
W E
S

Cloud-shrouded Kaupō Gap near Loʻaloʻa Heiau

28. Loʻaloʻa Heiau–
Sacrificial heiau at Kaupō

THIS LARGE *heiau*, at 510 by 100 feet, with 30-foot-high walls, has many small altars on the top platform, giving it a fortlike appearance. The *heiau* is ancient and was reputedly built by the *menehune* for the ancient gods. Stones for the *heiau* came from fifteen miles away. Archaeologist Emory related seeing small footprints in the lava about thirteen miles away from the *heiau*, and local residents informed him that the footprints were made by *menehune* walking through burning lava. The residents theorized that the footprints were embedded deeply because the stones that the *menehune* carried were so heavy. The small, child-sized footprints ran every which way and in circles.

Later, the *heiau* in the Kaupō area were used as war *heiau*, and sacrificial victims were offered to the gods by the High Chief Kekaulike. He is said to have delighted in war and gathered his warriors and canoes here as he prepared to attack the island of Hawaiʻi. He was defeated, but not before cutting down all the trees in Kona and slaughtering the country people of Kohala.

Kamehameha the Great also made offerings here to his war god Kū. The *heiau* was rededicated by Kamehameha's son, Liholiho, when the latter was still a child. It is interesting to note that Liholiho's full name was Ka-lani-nui-kua-liholiho-i-ke-*kapu* (the great chief with the burning-back taboo), referring to the taboo against approaching him from the back. The punishment for breaking this taboo was death.

There is a story that on these slopes with their many *heiau*, a high priest decried the overthrow of the *kapu* system and the abandonment of the gods, prophesying that it would result in the extinction of the order. In distress and despair, he disrobed in front of the people and foretold his own death, which occurred mysteriously the next day.

(References: Kamakau 1992, 65, 66; Pukui, Elbert, and Mookini 1989, 133; Sterling 1998, 173, 174.)

The lava fields around the narrow, twisting Kaupō Road hold many burial caves and heiau. The family lands of Jacob Mau lie here. Jacob told us that his uncle, as a young boy, found a secret burial cave. He was not afraid or superstitious and went inside to explore. He left with two items: a tortoise shell comb and a small pipe. He hid the stolen items under his bed.

That night his father shook him awake. "What do you have, that you should not have?" he asked.

"Nothing."

"Yes you do. Something is here that shouldn't be here, and someone wants it."

The boy waited until his father was asleep and then took the comb and pipe and tiptoed outside, burying them in the garden. When he returned to his bedroom, he glanced in the mirror. He saw a girl combing her long hair and an old man smoking a pipe. He screamed and screamed, and his father rushed in.

The father made his son walk back the two miles to the burial cave that very night. He followed on his horse, carrying a kerosene lamp. They replaced the items and apologized to the spirits.

Jacob says that when he and his uncle went hunting in the area recently, his uncle pointed out the burial cave and reminded him of the strange experience.

28. Loʻaloʻa Heiau

Large platform of Loʻaloʻa Heiau with sweeping views of valley and sea

Directions: Drive the hair-raising road five miles from the secret pool (Site 27) to the store at Kaupō. Just before the store is a narrow road with fourteen mailboxes beside it. Follow this road *mauka* (toward the mountains) for about one mile until you see a small house on your left. Go through the gate on the opposite side of the road. The *heiau* is across the field and slightly downhill about three hundred yards, and it is enclosed by barbed wire. This is private property, and you should first ask the rangers at Kīpahulu if it is permissible to visit the *heiau*; tel. (808) 248-7375. At the time of this writing, the rangers were not certain whether this land had been acquired as part of the Haleakalā National Park.

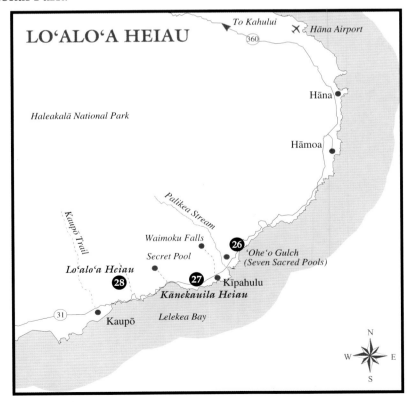

Great Day Trips
and Places to Stay on Maui

Drive 1. Take the walking tour of Lahaina (Site 20) in the morning, and visit Pu'u Keka'a (Black Rock) (Site 19) and its beautiful underwater world in the afternoon.

Great Places to Stay: The historic town of Lahaina is a whirlwind of activity and happy people at night, and the Ohana Maui Islander, 660 Wainee Street, Lahaina, supplies a quiet, comfortable place to recoup. The activities desk will supply you with a map of the historic walking tours of Lahaina. For more information call (800) 367-5226 or (808) 667-9766. (Rates: moderate)

The coast at Kā'anapali is full of excellent resorts, and the Sheraton-Maui at Black Rock is a beautiful place to stay. The beach and snorkeling are great. Watch the athletic youth carrying a fiery torch as he scrambles up Black Rock and does a swan dive into the ocean at sunset. For more information call (800) 325-3535 or (808) 661-0031. (Rates: expensive)

Drive 2. Haleakalā Volcano (Site 23) is a memorable experience. You will need a full day to visit the volcano.

Drive 3. Hāna is worth visiting for at least a day or two. Explore Pi'ilanihale Heiau (Site 24), Wai'ānapanapa Cave (Site 25), Seven Sacred Pools and the secret pool (Sites 26 and 27). The bamboo forest is a wonderful place to hike. Continue on to the faraway places of Kaupō (Site 28).

Hāna Plantation Houses. Ask for the three-bedroom house opposite the Queen's Pool and pretend you're an *ali'i* with a private ocean pool for your morning swim. For more information call (800) 657-7723 or (808) 248-7868. (Rates: moderate)

Hotel Hāna-Maui, with its friendly staff and beautiful airy, earth-toned rooms, is a luxurious place to stay or to dine. For more information call (800) 321-HANA or (808) 248-8211. (Rates: expensive)

Author at Blue Pool

Maui

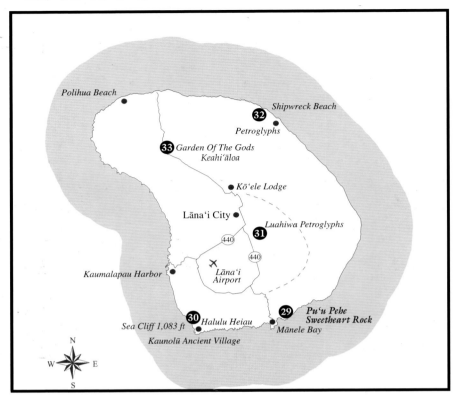

29. Pu'u Pehe Cove-
A rock for sweethearts

Where are you, O Pu'u Pehe?
Are you in the cave of Malauea?
Shall I bring you sweet water?
The water of the mountain?
Shall I bring the 'uwa'u bird?
The pala fern and the 'ōhelo berry?

You are baking the honu
And the red, sweet hala
Shall I pound the kalo of Maui?
Shall we dip in the gourd together?
The bird and the fish are bitter

Pu'u Pehe, a rock for sweethearts

And the mountain water is sour.
I shall drink it no more;
I shall drink it with 'Aipuhi,
The great shark of Mānele.
-Hawaiian chant (Emory 1969, 16)

PU'U PEHE, an eighty-foot-high rock island shaped by the ocean, stands in the calm blue waters of Pu'u Pehe Cove. A legend says that Pu'u Pehe, a young girl from Maui, was captured by a young warrior from Lāna'i as "the joint prize of love and war." Her beauty stunned him, and his fear of losing her led him to keep her in lonely places. One day, leaving her to prepare food in the sea cave of Malauea, he set out to fill his gourd with sweet water. As he returned, he saw a Kona storm approaching the coast. Frantically, he ran the three miles down the slope to rescue his wife, but the waves had dashed into the cave, drowning her. In grief, the young warrior retrieved her body and buried it on the rock island.

Lāna'i

Closeup of Pu'u Pehe

He then leapt into the sea below, taking his own life.

This beautiful little sandy cove is excellent for swimming and snorkeling, and high waves are not common.

Directions: Down the road from Mānele Bay Hotel at Hulopo'e Beach Park, walk five minutes along the dirt trail, past the picnic tables on the left side of the park, to Pu'u Pehe Cove.

(See map page 94)

Mānele Bay Hotel

29. Pu'u Pehe Cove

30. Kaunolū, Halulu Heiau, and Kahekili's Leap-
Ancient Evel Knievel stunt

> *O, my god, thou hast failed me!*
> *Thou didst promise life.*
> *Thy worshippers were to be as a forest,*
> *To fall only by the ax in battle.*
> *Had it been the god Turanga,*
> *That liar! I would not have trusted him.*
> *Like him, YOU are a man-eater!*
> *May thy mouth be covered with dung.*
> *Slush it over and over!*
> *This god is but a man-eater after all!*
>
> *. . . . .*
>
> *Plaster him well, friends. Ha! Ha!*
> *Dung is fit food for such gods!*
> *-Hawaiian chant (Luomala 1986, 66)*

Lāna'i

LĀNAʻI WAS once known as the "island of ghosts." Its earliest inhabitants were said to be man-eating spirits and fiendish, blood-curdling ghouls controlled by a sorceress, Pahulu. Hawaiians avoided Lānaʻi until the fifteenth century, when the ghosts were tricked and banished by Kaululāʻau, a prince from Maui.

Kaululāʻau was a spoiled child. His *aliʻi* father had ordered all boys born on the same day as his son to grow up as playmates with him in Lahaina. Unfortunately, Kaululāʻau was destructive and mischievous. When he and his companions pulled up breadfruit trees by their roots, he was banished to Lānaʻi by a *kahuna*. He was expected to die there, killed by the spirits, but night after night his father saw his fire on the beach. Eventually, the father sent his warriors to investigate. The spirits were gone. Kaululāʻau, with courage and ingenuity, had saved Lānaʻi. He became a hero, and families in Lānaʻi are proud to trace their genealogies back to him.

The ancient village of Kaunolū was built at a bay that provided excellent fishing and anchorage for canoes. Scattered down the cliffs and surrounded by *kiawe* trees, there are eighty-six platforms that once were dwellings. The cool, dry caves held food. Rocks and animal and human bones provided material for tools, weapons, and fishing equipment. *Pili* grass was used to thatch huts. Noni trees provided medicine, and coconut trees provided food and milk. The outer fibers of the coconut provided cordage. Dog teeth were used for anklets and whale bone for pendants for festive occasions.

The site of Halulu Heiau, a place of refuge, is well chosen. The *heiau* is located on a point on the western side of Kaunolū Gulch, and it dominates the landscape. It is surrounded on three sides by sheer, high sea cliffs. The ocean entering Kolo-kolo cave makes an eerie rumbling sound that seems to come from below the *heiau*. This was a *luakini heiau* where Kamehameha I held ceremonies. Since the chiefs were often in danger of being overthrown, a small military outlook was a necessity. A tower provided an unobstructed view of the gulch and sea, and a conch shell trumpet was used to sound a warning.

This was predominantly a fishing village, and life revolved around the sea and its resources. The bay was regarded as sacred because of its exceptional fishing. A fisherman in old Hawaiʻi was an honored person, as fishing was a skilled occupation, demand-

30. Kaunolū, Halulu Heiau

Lāna'i's high cliffs from Kahekili's Leap

ing knowledge of the stars, winds, currents, and clouds.

Kapu was observed when fishermen prepared their fishing gear, and while they lashed their hooks no one was allowed to make any noise, or run in and out, or talk to the fishermen. Fishermen today would appreciate this respect! A fisherman's wife could not gossip or tell neighbors that her husband was fishing. Fishing grounds were preserved and declared *kapu* at different times of the year. To ensure the cooperation of the elements, fishermen made an offering of the first catch of the day to the fishing god. The least prized fish of the day was the *weke*. The spirit of the sorceress Pahulu was said to have entered this fish, and some species contained a substance that produced terrible nightmares.

The sacred fish idol of Kamehameha I once stood on an altar in the gulch below the *heiau*, and it still lies hidden somewhere here. Tradition says that the man responsible for its care mishandled it and, as a consequence, died.

Petroglyphs of human and animal forms, even one of a surfer, are carved in the clumps of smooth boulders in several areas on the western ridge.

Kahekili, a fearsome warrior with tattoos covering the whole right side of his face and body, controlled Lāna'i in the late eighteenth century. Kahekili's Leap is a sixty-two-foot-high cliff west of the *heiau*, at the very edge of the precipice. Here the chief's

bravest soldiers would, at his command, test their courage and leap into the sea. Some managed to clear the fifteen-foot-wide ledge that protrudes below, while others entered the spirit world, leaving their broken bodies on the rocks.

This area is a rich archaeological source, and fishermen's tools can still be found here today. Archaeologists from the Bishop Museum studied the site in 1994, and there is an interpretive trail from the parking lot to guide visitors through the ruins. (References: Emory 1969, 51-60, 97-104; Fornander 1917-20, 4: 488; Gay 1965; Kirch 1985, 134; Malo 1996, 208-13.)

A Hawaiian friend, Buddy Peters, told us that one of his ancestors was chief fisherman for Kamehameha I. To be the King's fisherman was considered a prestigious position. His grandfather was also a skilled fisherman, and every morning he would stand looking at the ocean, assessing the fishing for the day. He would lean on a particular rock, because it was comfortable to lean on and because it was in a shady place. The rock acquired the reputation of being a fishing god. People would say "Look, he is praying to that rock," when he was just enjoying the view of the ocean and a break from his wife.

30. Kaunolū, Halulu Heiau

Directions: It is difficult to drive to the village, as some landowners have placed barbed wire gates across previously used roads. We were lucky to have Sol Kaho'ohalahala, Cultural Director, and Bonnie Phelps, Public Relations Coordinator, from the Lāna'i Company show us an alternative route and take us through the ancient village that they are helping to preserve.

Prepare for a wild ride! The extremely rough, bone-jarring dirt road is accessible by four-wheel drive only-it requires navigating through gulches right in the middle of the road. Drive on Highway 440 toward Kaumalapau Harbor, past the airport turnoff. Take a sharp left on the first dirt trail and proceed on the straight, "smooth" trail a couple of miles to a yellow standpipe on your right. Turn right and follow the cavernous trail slowly down the hill toward the ocean and Kaunolū. There are two parking areas, one farther down the hill from the interpretive trail. The village is very interesting and the cove is beautiful, with intensely red cliffs and a very blue sea. Take water and sunscreen

(See map page 94)

Rocky outcropping separated from the headland

31. Luahiwa Petroglyphs-
Art gallery for royalty

O, Kāne and Lono! Gods of the husbandmen,
Give life to the land!
Until there is food to waste,
Until it sprouts thickly in the ground,
And the shade of the leaves covers all.
May the bounteousness of food come
From you, O Kāne and Lono,
It is spoken. The kapu is released.
-Hawaiian chant (Handy and Handy 1991, 581)

THE TINY island of Lāna'i has great significance in the Hawaiian Islands as the landing site of the gods. According to mythology, the ancient god Kū, his wife, Hina, and later the god Kāne all landed here. The Sacred Crater-a huge volcanic crater-was the birthplace of the creative forces that formed the island.

A rain *heiau*, located in a cluster of stones carved with numerous petroglyphs, was dedicated to the gods who symbolized fertility of the land and the race. A large boulder here with many scattered images is believed to possess the power of Hina, and another in the forest uplands is said to possess the power of Kū. Farmers called upon these gods for rain and abundant crops.

Ancient Hawaiians left their picture albums for us here; a double-hulled canoe sails on for centuries, and warriors show off their weapons. In 1870 Hawaiian students from Lahainaluna school on Maui carved cats, dogs, horses, and men on the rocks.

In 1861 Walter Murray Gibson, a charismatic figure, pursued his dream of an island utopia here. After failing in the East Indies and landing in a Dutch prison, he arrived in Lāna'i as a Mormon, the High Priest of Melchizedek and the chosen emissary of Mormon President Brigham Young. Gibson entered enthusiastically into his role as the father of Lāna'i but was eventually excommunicated by the Mormon church for claiming equal authority as Brigham Young, diverting funds to buy land in his own name instead of the church's name, and also for encouraging "vicious practices" such as hula dancing.

The Mormons left to establish their very successful settlement at Lā'ie on O'ahu. Gibson, maintaining a firm hold on the lands he had acquired, proceeded on with a plan to bring "ruined yet energetic" planters and freed men from the newly reconstructed South. He developed a sheep and goat ranch in the Luahiwa Crater area, then, bored with the bucolic life, he moved to Honolulu. He became prime minister to King Kalākaua and owner of a newspaper defending the Hawaiian Kingdom against the eventual takeover of government by business leaders. He commissioned the statue of King Kamehameha I and provided the down payment for the construction of 'Iolani Palace. He was responsible for bringing the Franciscan order of nuns to Honolulu to nurse the lepers, and fell in love with the sweet Mother Marianne, the patient Mother Superior.

In many ways, he was revolutionary with his ideas and well ahead of his time. He became involved in so many issues that he was called "The Minister of Everything." The business interests opposed his high-spending budget deficits and his attempts to create a Commonwealth of the Pacific with Hawai'i as its hub.

They were frantic with his plan to organize a two-million-dollar loan and his minting of the first Hawaiian coin to back it. In spite of his influence in the islands he loved, there is no street or building named after Gibson. He had made the mistake of offending the victors.
(Reference: Adler and Kamins 1986.)

Directions: From Lāna'i City, head toward Mānele Bay on Mānele Road (Highway 440), and as you descend from a partial forest to an open basin area, turn left on the first dirt road. Head straight for the large water tank clearly visible on the hill. The large boulders with petroglyphs are past the tank on the slopes of the hill. Sadly, vandals have also carved their names here, and the boulders have been blackened from a recent forest fire. The steep slopes are very slippery, and limited funding has prevented Sol Kaho'ohalahala, whose ambition it is to protect the fragile sites of Lāna'i, from building a trail to protect the petroglyphs and assist visitors. He hopes to accomplish this in the near future.

31. Luahiwa Petroglyphs

32. Shipwreck Beach Petroglyphs-
Birdman of Lāna'i

LITTLE STICK FIGURES about twelve inches tall, with strange, birdlike heads, decorate the rocks on the lonely and windswept shores of Shipwreck Beach. Their meaning is a mystery lost in time.

Route 440 to Shipwreck Beach crosses desolate plains, passes misty, pine-clad mountains, and gives panoramic views of the coast. This coast has been the graveyard for many vessels-look for the rusty hulk of a World War II Liberty Ship stranded on the reef. On the dark nights of the moon, ghosts of ancient warriors have been seen and heard along the shoreline road, and sounds of wailing and babies crying haunt many areas of the coast.
(References: Bisignani 1994, 327-28; Emory 1969.)

Chris and Lew Trusty, professional writer and photographer, camped here one dark night. In the middle of the night Chris was awakened by the sound of a huge crowd of people walking through the crackling under-growth. She could hear the murmur of many voices. Leaping up, she went to the opening of the tent, and looking into the distance, saw the glow of lights coming from the forest of kiawe trees. Lew also heard the loud rustling noise, and deciding there was no way they could spend the night there, they packed up and left as quickly as they could. They had only recently arrived in Hawai'i and had never heard of night marchers, but this seemed the wisest thing to do.

Directions: You need a four-wheel-drive vehicle for most travel in Lāna'i. From the Lodge at Kō'ele drive past the parking lot to the top of the hill and proceed straight ahead on Route 440 for 8.5 miles over the mountains. As you descend the mountain, you can see the World War II Liberty Ship resting on the reef to your left. Near the sea, the dirt road to the left passes through kiawe trees and becomes a sandy road (signs are not a strong feature here). About three miles farther, there are small primitive fishing cabins. A short walk leads to the ruins of a lighthouse, and an arrow on a sign for "The Bird Man of Lāna'i" points you to the petroglyphs. This is a good place for beach-combers seeking glass fishing floats.

(See map page 94)

32. Shipwreck Beach

33. Keahiʻāloa-
Fires of a powerful kahuna and a garden of the gods

Sunset at Keahiʻāloa, Garden of the Gods

> *The fire burns, the fire of the night, of Lanipili,*
> *Where is the fire, the fire of the night, of Lanipili?*
> *In the heavens, death in the heavens,*
> *Decaying in the heavens, beset by maggots in the heavens,*
> *Moldy in the heavens, reduced to ashes in the heavens,*
> *The death of the kāhuna ʻanāʻanā with the bait,*
> *Oh Kāne, fire of Kū, of the fire, the brightness appears,*
> *Fiery in the passing of time, roaring aloud of the fire.*
> -Hawaiian *kāhuna* chant (Malo 1996, 205)

THIS IS a strange and otherworldly badlands of twisted lava, yellow, orange, and purple pinnacles, and giant boulders sculpted by the raging forces of nature. Why is this area completely denuded of trees? Possibly because of the once perpetual fires.

The nearby area of Kaʻā (The Burning) was once well populated. Kawelo, a powerful *kahuna*, was responsible for keeping alight a perpetually burning fire, and the area was known as Keahiʻāloa (The Long-lasting Fire). The *kāhuna* had assured the

Strange rock formations and colored landscape- Keahi'āloa

people that supplies of pigs and dogs would never cease as long as the people brought fuel for the fire and dogs and pigs to feed the *kāhuna*.

Kawelo noticed that many of his subjects were under some sort of supernatural spell. A council meeting of elders decided that the Moloka'i *kahuna*, Lanikāula, was responsible for the spell. Kawelo went to Moloka'i with the intention of disposing of Lanikāula.

Feigning friendship, he spied on Lanikāula and noticed that Lanikāula safeguarded his excrement from other sorcerers by burying it on the small island of Mokuho'oniki. Secretly, Kawelo followed Lanikāula. He scooped out the inside of a potato and filled the skin with the excrement. Then, triumphantly, he returned to Lāna'i and burned the excrement in a fire lit with *kukui* nuts. The smoke from the fire burning the excrement changed the color of the lehua flowers to purple.

When Lanikāula saw the blue flames, he knew that he was doomed to die. Before he died, however, he prophesied the death of his enemy. This prophesy proved correct. Kawelo, on returning to Lāna'i, discovered that his daughter had neglected to keep alight the sacred fires. She had been preoccupied that moonlit night with her young lover. In shame and disgrace, Kawelo jumped to his death from a precipice off Maunalei. Archaeologist Gibson states that many natives of Lānaʻi believed that their dogs and hogs passed away in consequence of the fires dying.

Lonely trails lead to Kaʻena Point, a desolate shore. By 1835 Protestant missionaries from Lahaina began paying regular visits to Lānaʻi. Upset by some of the carefree sexual activity in Lahaina, they established a penal colony for adulterous women at Kaʻena Point on Lānaʻi, and another on Kahoʻolawe for male offenders. The offenders are said to have visited each other, and the sentences of all were ultimately commuted when they were rescued in 1837 in an outrigger canoe from Lahaina.

Lānaʻi's largest *heiau*, Kaʻena Iki, stood on this coast, shadowed by the dark sea cliffs.

(References: Emory 1969, 18; Gay 1965, 59-64; Summers 1971, 156, 157.)

Directions: From the Lodge at Kōʻele proceed past the parking lot and two plantation houses on your right. Take the next dirt road on the left, where there is a sign for the "Garden of the Gods." About one hundred yards farther you will come to a T intersection. Turn right and proceed for about 6.4 miles. You will pass through Kānepuʻu Preserve. The road is well maintained. Visit at sunset to see the shifting colors of the rocks.

Silhouettes at sunset

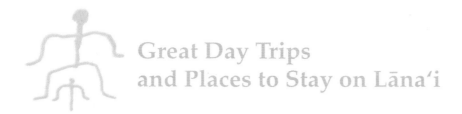

Drive 1. Clench your knuckles, grit your teeth, and take your four-wheel drive on a memorable trip to Kaunolū Ancient Village and Kahekili's Leap (Site 30). In the afternoon, explore Shipwreck Beach (Site 32). Have a cool drink at the Lodge at Kō'ele, set in the pine-covered highlands of Lāna'i.

Drive 2. Four-wheel drive it to the mystic world of ancient *kāhuna* and perpetual fires, known as Keahi'āloa, but dubbed the Garden of the Gods (Site 33). Enjoy rare Hawaiian dry-land forest and watch for tiny axis deer.

Drive 3. Visit Mānele Bay and walk to picturesque Pu'u Pehe Cove (Site 29). On the way, take a look at Luahiwa Petrogylphs. (Site 31).

There are very few car rentals on Lāna'i, so book ahead. Dollar Rent a Car supplies great four-wheel-drive jeeps; call (800) 800-4000.

Great Places to Stay: The romantic Mānele Bay Hotel, awash in soft colors and surrounded by gardens of flowers and waterfalls, is one of those impossibly beautiful resorts often found in Hawai'i. The sugar-white sandy cove is perfect for sunbathing, and snorkeling in the sparkling marine reserve is great too-Mānele Bay and Hulopo'e Bay have virtually undisturbed coral reefs. Golfers can try the signature hole at the championship golf course, a two-hundred-yard tee shot across the Pacific Ocean from a cliff 150 feet above the crashing surf. Lunch on the airy veranda of the resort, and you may see dolphins traveling by. For more information call (808) 565-7700. (Rates: expensive)

     The Hotel Lāna'i, right in the middle of small pine-clad Lāna'i City, has island old-style ambiance. Call (808) 565-7211. (Rates: inexpensive)

Keahi'āloa

Lāna'i

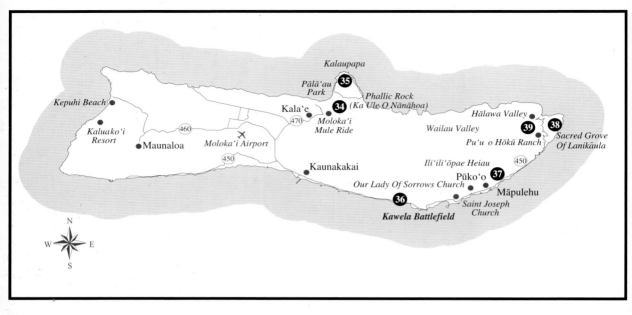

34. Kauleonānāhoa, Pālā'au State Park- *Phallic rock, fertility site*

There is life in the stone and death in the stone.
-old Hawaiian proverb (Gutmanis 1986)

THE SHAPE of this amazing stone clearly demonstrates what its probable powers are. This is a legendary fertility tool, a six-foot-high natural stone standing erect in a dense grove of ironwood trees. Standing just below the base of Nānāhoa Hill, this rock is also called "The Penis of Nānāhoa," and island women still come here to pray for fertility. We met a woman who had given birth to twins after visiting the site and asking for a child.

Archaeologists have found other stones in this area that are carved to resemble female genitals. These stones were taken to Nānāhoa to receive *mana* then taken home to make the land fertile.

Legend says that if a woman goes to Kauleonānāhoa with offerings and spends the night there, she will return home pregnant. The historian Coelho tells of a time when the people lacked off-spring because of fighting between husbands and wives. A *kahuna* advised the women to take offerings and sleep at the stone. When

Kauleonānāhoa (Phallic Rock), fertility site

they went home, all of the women were pregnant-they all had bundles to carry home.

Adjacent boulders to the north and northeast, downhill from the phallic rock, have phallic petroglyphs on them.

Directions: Head west from Kaunakakai on Highway 450. Turn north on Highway 470 and proceed to the parking lot at the end of the highway. The short trail to the phallic rock starts here.

Moloka'i

35. Kalaupapa National Historical Park- *Former leper colony*

> *At a blow, and with the price of his life, he made the place illustrious and public. If ever a man brought reforms, and died to bring them, it was he. It brought money, public interest, and best of all, it brought personal and caring supervision in the form of Brother Joseph Dutton, and the Sisters of the Franciscan Convent of St. Anthony of Syracuse, New York.*
> -Robert Louis Stevenson's summary of Father Damien in his Open Letter to the Reverend Dr. Hyde, Honolulu, 1880

THE KALAUPAPA peninsula, a long tongue of lava, reaches out into the swirling seas at the foot of dark 1,700-foot-high sea cliffs. From 1865 to 1974, more than eleven thousand lepers were exiled to these remote, lonely shores and left to die here. There were no houses, no hospitals, no doctors or nurses to care for the helpless. Kalaupapa was called "The Place of the Living Dead," and boatloads of new arrivals, often simply pushed overboard into the waves to struggle alone to the shore, were greeted with the phrase "In this place there is no law." The strong ruled here. Bands of men, desperate in this enforced isolation, plundered and raped the new arrivals, who included toddlers, teenagers, the middle-aged, and the elderly, often unfortunates who still showed few signs of the awful disease that would ultimately ravage them. Food was scarce, and the helpless died of starvation. Death was the only release from Kalaupapa.

In 1873 a young Catholic priest, Father Damien, arrived from Belgium. His mission in life was to aid and give succor to the lepers. He lived with them, fed them, bathed their wounds, and built shelters with his own hands. He walked up the steep cliffs to beg for food and clothing, and he petitioned church groups for aid. Conditions slowly improved at Kalaupapa. Finally Damien contracted leprosy. He told his congregation this fact when he started his sermon with the words, "We lepers…." By the time he died, in 1889, he knew that his people would be cared for. Father Damien is one of Hawai'i's most beloved heroes.

Leprosy, or Hansen's Disease, is now curable, and treatment renders the disease noncontagious. Former patients still live in Kalaupapa today; the average age is about seventy. They are assured lifetime occupancy of the park and are free to leave and return to their homes.

The best way to go to Kalaupapa is on the back of a mule. These dudes may be stubborn and pretty definite about which way they prefer to go, but trust them, they do know the way around all twenty-six switchbacks on the 1,700-foot downhill trail. The view of the sea cliffs is spectacular.

Saint Joseph's Church built by Father Damien in 1869

A bus driven by the sheriff, who is a former patient, takes you on a tour of the peninsula. Some one hundred people still live at Kalaupapa, but they stay in their homes and do not mingle with visitors. Recently a film on the life of Father Damien was made, and the patients appeared in it. The guide said they were looking forward to seeing themselves on the big screen.

Directions: A trail to Kalaupapa Lookout starts from the parking lot of Pālā'au State Park. The mule ride needs to be booked in advance; call (800) 567-7550 or (808) 567-6088. To fly or hike in call Damien Tours at (808) 567-6171.

(See map page 112)

36. Kawela Battlefield-
Night marchers' right-of-way

THE EASTERN half of Moloka'i is lush and green. Kamehameha V Highway, between the 6 and 15 - mile markers, winds around the coast, twisting between ancient blue fishponds and mountain gorges. Within this region, the Kawela Battlefield was the scene of a terrible battle in 1736, when invading O'ahu forces fought the combined forces of Moloka'i and Hawai'i. The Moloka'i chiefs had difficulty competing with the more powerful O'ahu forces, but they had the advantage of sorcery in overcoming their enemies. The O'ahu chief was killed and his forces were routed. Fornander describes this famous battlefield as a place where "the bones of the slain are the sports of the winds that sweep over that sandy plain, and cover or uncover them, as the case may be." He says that judging by the multitude of bones and skulls lying bleaching in the sun, the number of people that fought may be reckoned in the thousands.

In 1794 Kamehameha I stopped off on his way to conquer O'ahu and occupied Moloka'i. His canoes were drawn up for four miles along the shore. His ultimate war prize was a young bride, the sacred Keōpūolani (see Site 22).

The many fishponds, shimmering in the sun, tell a happier story of a novel way of arranging a constant supply of fresh fish. Underground springs supplied constant fresh water to the ponds, and the natural bottom of the area was unspoiled by silt. Fast runners supplied the chiefs with a fresh fish of the day. A *mo'o*, or dragon lizard, is said to have inhabited the ponds, so the fishermen had to be careful. This was, however, supposed to be a friendly *mo'o* who defended Moloka'i against a predatory shark. (Reference: Summers 1971, 91-92.)

We perched happily on bar stools in the cool, tropical ambiance of the open-air restaurant at the Hotel Moloka'i and discussed night marchers. Apparently the whole region between the 6 and 15-mile markers is full of them. Lyndon de la Cruz, the bartender and a great storyteller, told us of his personal experiences with these visitors from another dimension. One night when he and his friends were camping at the shore near the 13-mile marker, he woke to feel something crushing his chest. Lifting his head with a struggle, he saw a procession of night marchers passing through the tent. He and his friends could hear talking and laughing, which grew fainter as the warriors made their way to the shore. The campers huddled together, frightened and amazed, until morning.

Lyndon's neighbor, whose house is on the path of the night marchers, simply leaves the front and back doors open on the nights they march. He says that saves him from being bothered by them.

We sipped our cold wine and listened, fascinated. A Japanese-restaurant owner, David, sitting next to us at the bar, shook his head. "You shouldn't pay attention to these things," he said. "I, myself, simply ignore them. When they walk through my beach house and go to their canoes, I just think they can't harm me because I believe in God."

"But do you actually see them?" I asked.

"Oh yes," he replied. "I see them, carrying their torches. They walk by, laughing and making a noise. You can hear them coming from a long way away. They're going to their canoes. I just don't pay any attention to them."

Directions: The village of Kawela is 6 miles from Kaunakakai. At about the 13-mile marker (look for the sign for 'Ualapu'e Fishpond), a turnoff toward the sea takes you to a splendid fishpond with sluice gates opening to the ocean.

(See map page 112)

'Ualapu'e Fishpond, one of many ancient fishponds on Moloka'i

36. Kawela Battlefield

Stone platform of 'Ili'ili'ōpae Heiau was a school for sorcerers (photo credit State Parks Division of DLNR)

37. 'Ili'ili'ōpae Heiau–
School for sorcerers

For a life, a death,
A great ka'upu bird is calling out.
Sounding nearby, calling out.
What is the food it is calling for?
A man is the food it is calling for.
Thunder cracks in the heavens,
The earth quakes.
-"Pule Kāholo," Hawaiian *kāhuna* chant (Kamakau 1964, 125)

Numbness, numbness, numbness, numbness,
Spreads, spreads, spreads, spreads,
Stiffens, stiffens, stiffens, stiffens;
Your head droops, droops, droops,
Bends over, bends over,
It droops, droops.
-"Pule 'Umi Ho'ana," Hawaiian kāhuna chant (Kamakau 1964, 126)

THIS DARK, desecrated *heiau*, with a 286-by-87-foot stone platform, was renowned for its powerful *kāhuna* and sorcerers, whose chants mingled with the cries of humans being sacrificed. Commoners avoided this *heiau* and even other *kāhuna* feared it. Moloka'i was known as Pule o'o (Powerful Prayer), and the *heiau* was a school for sorcery where the *kāhuna* of Moloka'i and other islands were tutored.

Waterworn stones used to build the temple were passed hand-to-hand in a human chain over the mountains on the treacherously steep Wailau Trail, which begins just behind the *heiau*. Wooden idols representing Kūkā'ilimoku, Lono and Uli, archgoddess of sorcery, stood on the platform.

Reverend Forbes, an early missionary, related that from the twenty-fourth to the twenty-seventh day of the moon-the nights of Kāne-people were summoned to the temple by the beating of drums and loud shouting. Men gathered at the base of the temple. Women were kept out of sight. At a signal from the priests, all fell down on the ground, and the human sacrifice was carried in, tied to a scaffold, and strangled. Chanting continued throughout the ceremony.

Legend tells of a *kahuna* called Kamalo who lost his nine sons when they were sacrificed at the *heiau*, accused by the sorcerers of desecrating the temple drum. Kamalo sought revenge. He prayed to his *'aumakua*, the shark god, who sent a flash flood that washed the sorcerers into the sea, where the shark god then devoured them.

The ten-minute walk from the main road to the *heiau* is very pretty and shady. The owners of the house at the trail end have numerous biblical warnings in their garden advising repentance, and there was a "please take one" sign on their mailbox, which held interesting pamphlets, including Nelson Mandela's inaugural speech.

(Reference: Summers 1971, 130-34.)

View of the heiau's eastern wall from the stream

Directions: Head east of Kaunakakai toward Hālawa Valley. Just after the 14-mile marker there's a warrior sign, and a gated trail leads to the *heiau*, which is a ten-minute walk away. Watch for a sign on your left at the end of the trail; you have to cross the small stream to see the *heiau*. At the back of the *heiau* is the trailhead for the cross-island trek into Wailau Valley. It leads to a 2,800-foot-high *pali*, and the way down is treacherous and unmarked. The Sierra Club hikes here occasionally.

(See map page 112)

*The Sacred Grove of Lanikāula,
a prophet's secret burial place*

38. Sacred Grove of Lanikāula-
Bewitched burial site

*A great owl calls out,
Whistling as it calls.
What is the food it is calling for?
A man is the food it is calling for.
Thunder cracks in the heavens,
The earth quakes, the lightning flashes.
Your legs bend,
Your hands become paralyzed,
Your back hunches,
Your neck is twisted,
Your chin is crooked,
Your eyes are sunken,
Disease has broken into the brain,
Your liver rots,*

Your intestines fall to pieces.
-"Pule Kāholo" ("Praying to Death"), Hawaiian *kāhuna*
chant (Kamakau 1964, 125)

THIS IS the burial site of a great and feared prophet; take care not to offend him! The grave lies hidden in a sacred grove of *kukui* trees on Pu'u o Hoku (Hill of the Night of the Full Moon) Ranch. Many Hawaiians regard the grave as a place of great power and *mana*. Lanikāula, a celebrated sixteenth century *kahuna* and prophet, had a reputation for counseling and sorcery that continues to this day. Lanikāula practiced powerful sorcery handed down from the sorceress Pahulu (see Site 30). Pilgrims came from all the islands to ask his advice.

Lanikāula's reputation was enhanced by his use of *Kālaipāhoa*, the greatly feared poisonwood gods. These sorcery gods were carved from the wood of poisonwood trees found at the summit of Mauna Loa, in the Kaluako'i District. Even a chip from the trees was said to be powerful enough to kill a man. Carvers of the trees had to practice extreme care!

Even great prophets sometimes meet their match, and Lanikāula, who foresaw the deaths of many, was unable to prevent the sorcery that led to his own demise. In spite of his powers, Lanikāula feared the sorcery of rival *kāhuna* and buried his excrement on Mokuho'oniki, a small offshore island, so that it could not be used in spells against him. Kawelo, a rival sorcerer from Lāna'i,

Island of Mokuho'oniki—
Lanikāula secretly buried
his excrement here

Moloka'i

visited Lanikāula and pretended friendship. He spied on Lanikāula and noted that Lanikāula paddled his canoe to Mokuhoʻoniki every day. He followed and dug up the excrement. He then hollowed out a sweet potato, placed the excrement in it, and told Lanikāula that he was returning to Lānaʻi. Lanikāula invited him to take more potatoes. Kawelo replied that one was all he needed. He burned the excrement in a ritual fire and prayed Lanikāula to death-some say by constipation.

When Lanikāula saw the blue and purple flames on the shores of Lānaʻi, he knew Kawelo had lit a ritual fire using oil from *kukui* nuts, and that he was going to be prayed to death. He instructed his sons to protect his body from his enemies by burying it in a secret grave so that his bones could not be found and their *mana* could not be used to control his spirit. He instructed them to plant a grove of *kukui* trees over the grave. He also prophesied the ruin of Kawelo. This prophecy came true. Pepe, Kawelo's daughter, absorbed in her young lover, allowed the sacred fire at Lānaʻi to burn out. Kawelo, distressed and afraid of the people's anger, jumped to his death over the precipice of Maunalei.

The tradition of the poisonwood tree gods lasted through the centuries. The mighty Kamehameha I had his own piece of a poisonwood god that he kept in a temple with its own *kahu* (keeper). He venerated the god as a protection against sorcery and prayed to it every morning and evening. It was said that even haoles (foreigners) felt the *mana* of the god.

Other chiefs fervently desired their own portion of the god, and after Kamehameha's death, a *Kālaipāhoa* image was cut into pieces and distributed among the chiefs. Bundles of nīoi wood were placed next to the god and were said to partake of the *mana* and become poisonous. They could then be used as "fetchers" in sorcery, sent out at night in the form of a streak of light, large at the head and tapering into a tail. Reports of sightings of these "fireballs" are common in Hawaiʻi, New Zealand and Tahiti. A poisonwood god-a fierce figure with slightly flexed knees, grasping fingers, and an open mouth-was on exhibit until recently in the Bishop Museum in Honolulu (at present, the artifact is in storage until claims for its return to the Hawaiian groups from which it originated are resolved).

In 1822, *kāhuna* attended a ritual ceremony held in Oʻahu by Chief Keʻeaumoku. The chief's wife had died and he believed

Sacred grove of kukui trees

that she had been prayed to death. A large fire was lit, the belief being that the face of the guilty person would appear in the flames. The *kāhuna* gazed into the fire, and all present stated that they saw the same face in the flames. They named a certain chief as the guilty party, although some felt regret because he was their master. The chief was sentenced to death by sorcery, and he soon died.
(Reference: Summers 1971, 156, 157, 198, 204.)

Moloka'i resident Anna Goodhue told us many interesting stories about the island. Anna is one of the oldest people on Moloka'i, although her beautiful face doesn't show that. She feels very close to the prophet Lanikāula, who protects her family.

Anna related that the grove of kukui trees planted by Lanikāula's sons was once the largest grove on the island. It was called Ulu Kukui o Lanikāula. In recent times, a well-liked couple named Brown bought the grove and gave great feasts there. Anna's daughter attended the feasts. The tables were arranged around Lanikāula's grave, and the prophet approved.

Land was leased to a farmer named Satara. When his watermelon crop flourished, he asked for more land, and then trouble arose. Mr. Brown gave permission, in spite of his wife's objections, to cut down part of the grove of kukui. As the first tree fell, Mr. Brown suffered a stroke and was paralyzed. No crops grew, and the farmer died in poverty.

Other neighbors related how workers cutting the trees became covered with rashes, and a bulldozer operator clearing the land overturned his machine into a sewage pool. Don't mess with a prophet's grave!

Directions: Go past Pūko'o on the road to Hālawa Valley. The overlook is about half a mile past the Pu'u o Hoku Ranch entrance. As the road climbs the hill, stop at the turnoff overlooking the first gulch after the ranch, and the grove of light-colored *kukui* trees can be seen across the gulch. The grove, on about five acres of land owned by the ranch, is maintained by Hawaiian *kūpuna*. Permission must be obtained from the ranch *manager* to go to the site. The ranch will at present allow visitors accompanied by a Hawaiian *kupuna* to the site. It is surrounded by a six-foot-high barbed-wire fence.

(See map page 112)

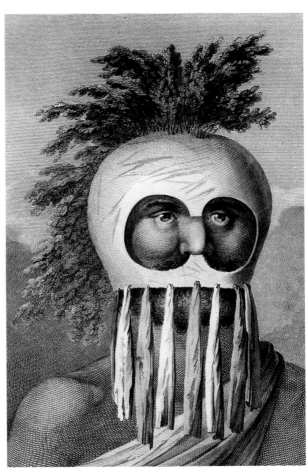

A man of the Sandwich Islands, in a gourd mask.
Courtesy: Hawai'i State Archives

38. Sacred Grove of Lanikāula

39. Hālawa Valley-
Valley of sorcerers

> *O Lono*
> *Listen to my voice*
> *Rush upon [name of victim] and enter,*
> *Enter and curl up,*
> *Curl up and straighten out.*
> - *kāhuna* death prayer instructing spirit slaves to enter the
> body of an intended victim and absorb the victim's life
> force (Steiger 1971, 54)

IN ANCIENT times the *kāhuna* of Moloka'i were feared as the most
powerful priests in the islands. Moloka'i had seventeen *heiau* built
for human sacrifice, nine of which were in the valley of Hālawa.
The largest, Mana Heiau, is situated high on the northern slopes of
the valley. Its stone platforms and terraces rise to thirteen feet but
are overgrown with vegetation.

The most powerful *kāhuna* lived in this valley. Their ancient mysticism was handed down from the sorceress Pahulu of Lānaʻi. These *kāhuna* had the power to pray men to death or to save them from the death spells of rival *kāhuna*. Obscure and deadly warfare was carried on between rival orders of sorcerers.

Chiefs from Oʻahu and Maui fought to control this agriculturally rich valley. Although Molokaʻi had a much smaller population than Maui or Oʻahu, it succeeded in resisting domination because of these greatly feared *kāhuna*. The local Molokaʻi chiefs used sorcery to defend themselves.

The *heiau* of Hālawa Valley were schools for young men desiring to become *kāhuna*, and students came from all the islands to learn powerful spells and sacred rites. They studied *ʻanāʻanā*, the art of praying to death. *Kāhuna* with this frightening skill could give hypnotic suggestions to prisoners of war or other unfortunates before the latter were executed, ordering them to serve the *kāhuna* as spirit slaves. The *kāhuna* would then control the spirit slaves and could send them out to possess the body of an enemy and absorb all his *mana*, causing his death. This was, naturally, greatly feared.

They also learned *hoʻo-piʻo-piʻo*, the use of sorcery to bring about death; *hoʻo-una-una*, the art of dispatching evil spirit entities on missions of death; *hoʻo-komo-komo*, the art of creating sickness; and *poʻi ʻuhane*, the entrapping of spirits. *Kilokilo ʻuhane* was a powerful means of extorting wealth from victims. A *kahuna* would, with bare-faced lying and shrewd conjecture, relate that he had seen the astral body of a certain person, entirely naked with his eyes staring wildly and his tongue hanging out. He would accuse the person of clubbing him with a stick until he was senseless. This was an ominous sign of the person's impending death, and it made the person eager to atone for his sins by compensating the *kahuna*.

The ancient *kāhuna* had other useful skills: *hana aloha*, love-inducing sorcery; and *kala aloha*, sorcery to free a victim from the power of the love-inducing sorcery. There was *nānā-uli*, the art of foretelling the weather; *lapaʻau*, healing with herbs or through prayers and instant healing of broken bones.

The students lived in a *moku hale*, a house set apart for training. Platforms remaining from these houses are in the valley. The work of learning the magical prayers of *pule ʻanāʻanā* was filthy, dangerous, and deadly. It was carried out under *kapu*. The students' hair was *kapu* and could not be cut, so their hair and beards became long and tangled. Water was *kapu*, so they could not wash. They could not touch women. Students studied and prayed all day, ate disgusting and poisonous foods, and controlled their bodies in all things.

Eventually, if accepted by the gods, they acquired many powers. They could concentrate on a cliff and it would fall, on a rock and it would crumble. They could make fire come out of rock, and cause whales and sharks to be cast up on land. They could remove afflictions sent by sorcery and cause the death of the one who had cast the spell. These were *kāhuna 'anā'anā*. Some wicked *kahuna* were called *kāhuna po'o ko'i* (adze heads), an insulting term for evil sorcerers, thus called because their

Hālawa Headland and beach

heads were shaped to resemble an adze, indicating that they were Kū practitioners. They took the possessions of others, including their wives, children, fish, and poi. They could inflict death, sickness, and paralysis. On dark, dank nights in ancient Hālawa Valley, the fires of *kāhuna* would blaze as they performed their rituals.

The people of Hālawa Valley were accomplished fishermen, and there are a number of fishing shrines here. Many families had shark *'aumākua*, or ancestral gods, to protect them when fishing. If a family had no such *'aumākua*, the *kāhuna* would help by placing the wrapped body of a dead family member in the ocean beside the shark god. The shark would accept the spirit of the deceased, and the family would then be related to the shark god. They could recognize their relative by the markings on the shark's body, which were the same as those on the cloth containing the corpse. They would claim protection from the shark god, and he would drive fish into shore for them. This belief in form transformation was called *kino lau*, and Hawaiians felt a close relationship with all of nature because of this belief.

Even today *kāhuna* go to Moloka'i to retrieve some of the lost arts and attempt to get in touch with ancient *'aumākua*. (References: Kamakau 1964, 123; Kirch 1985, 127-30; Malo 1996, 112, 113; McBride 1969; Summers 1971, 159-71.)

The road to Hālawa Valley is narrow, winding, and hair-raising. The views of tall waterfalls, curving beaches, thick jungles, and grassy plains are spectacular.

From Hālawa Valley, a muddy trail leads to two waterfalls. The three-mile round-trip hike passes many ancient walls, terraces, and platforms. The 250-foot-high Moa'ula Falls, splendidly cascading into first one huge pool and then another, is said to have a giant mo'o, or lizard woman, in the pool under the falls. Before swimming, be sure to test her mood by throwing a ti leaf into the water. If it floats, she won't bother you. If it sinks, she is in a bad mood and stirring up the currents below. Why chance it! Our guide, Ken Dudoit, believes that men with lizard-like markings all over their bodies actually lived in the cave next to the pool, which gave rise to the superstition.

Lush Hālawa Valley
and stream meet the sea

The hike is easier if you have a guide. Part of the land is private property, and the owners prefer that a local guide takes you through the taro fields. Our guide, Ken, of Waterfall Adventures, is very knowledgeable. He will tell you stories of the valley, make sure the river doesn't flood when you cross it, and warn you which trees (be-still, or nohomālie, a yellow oleander) cause deadly heart palpitations. Quite worthwhile knowledge!

39. Hālawa Valley

*Remote Hālawa Valley
with cascading waterfall.*

Moloka'i

Directions: Hālawa is thirty miles east of the airport at the end of Kamehameha Highway (Highway 450). Past Pūko'o, the road becomes quite spectacular and allows barely enough room for one vehicle. If you are unlucky enough to meet an oncoming vehicle, the 4,800-foot sheer drop is ample reason to pray for divine help.

The trail to Moa'ula Falls has been closed indefinitely to the public and there is no access without a guide. Check with Molokai Fish and Dive, Waterfall Adventures (808) 553-5926.

If the hike opens again to the public, the directions are as follows: Park at the turnout at the end of the road. Cross the road and walk up a dirt road past a small church and a group of houses. Take the right fork toward Hālawa Stream. Follow a white PVC water pipe that leads along the left bank of the stream. The trail passes under giant mango trees and at a rise, it forks. Take the left fork, and follow the trail on the right side of the stream past the remains of old taro patches and home sites. Follow the water pipe, listen for the falls, and follow the sound. You have to cross the stream to reach the falls. Be careful if it is raining, as flash floods can occur suddenly, and people have drowned here. And be sure to take mosquito repellant!

(See map page 112)

39. Hālawa Valley

Drive 1. The Phallic Rock (Site 34) and Kalaupapa Overlook (Site 35). The mule ride to the Kalaupapa Peninsula is a full day's trip that is very enjoyable. Call (808) 526-0888 for information.

Great Place to Stay: Kaluako'i Villas is a pleasant place to stay on Moloka'i's nicest beach. Most rooms have large lanais and pictur-esque views of the fairways or the ocean. There are two pretty coves for swimming and miles of coastal walking trails. For more information call the Kaluako'i Villas at (808) 552-2721. (Rates: moderate)

Drive 2. A wonderful drive east to Hālawa Valley (Site 39), stop-ping for: Night Marchers (Site 36), 'Ili'ili'ōpae Heiau (Site 37), and Sacred Grove of Lanikāula (Site 38). Arrange for a hike in the valley by calling Waterfall Adventures at (808) 553-5926.

Great Place to Stay: Hotel Moloka'i, Kaunakakai, has the look of a Polynesian village. Rooms are studios with large lanais and com-fortable furnishings. There is a friendly open-air restaurant and bar overlooking the pool and ocean. For more information contact the Hotel Moloka'i at (800) 535-0085 or (808) 553-5347. (Rates: inexpensive)

Sunset Beach · 83 · Kahuku · Lāʻie
Waimea Bay · **53** · Puʻu O Mahuka Heiau
Kaʻena Point · **40**
Kāneana Cave · 803 · 99 · **43** Kūkaniloko · Kualoa Ranch · **52**
41 · Kāneʻākī Heiau · Wahiawā · Mokoliʻi Island
Mākaha · **42** · Healing Stones · **44**
Keaīwa Heiau · **45**
ʻAiea · Kailua
51 Ulopō Heiau
Punchbowl National Cemetery · **46**
Punahou · Mānoa Chinese Cemetery
Honolulu Airport · Pōhakuloa · **49** · **48**
Waikīkī Beach · **47** · **50** Hanauma Bay
Wizard Stones
Diamond Head · Hawaiʻi Kai

40. Kaʻena Point, Waiʻanae District–
Leaping place of souls

> *Kaʻena, salty and barren*
> *Now throbs with the blaze of the sun;*
> *The rocks are consumed by the heat.*
> -Hawaiian chant (Emerson 1978, 104)

DESOLATE KAʻENA Point was known as a place from which souls departed from the earth. A large coral boulder, called *Leina a ka ʻuhane* (Soul's Leap), is located east of the lighthouse. This was a significant Hawaiian religious site. Here, the souls of the near dead, or the dead, wandered. Here they leaped into the night.

There are shattered remains of numerous *heiau* in the area, the first one just before Yokohama Beach. A soul first had to pass Keawaʻula, or Yokohama Beach, where his *ʻaumakua* decided if he was ready to go on to the next world. Good souls moved to the right when leaping; those who moved to the left fell into the "pit of endless night." On Oʻahu a person who died was spoken of as "having gone west."
(Reference: Sterling and Summers 1978, 92, 93.)

Directions: Proceed as far as you can go on Farrington Highway, past Mākaha to Yokohama Beach, where the paved road becomes a dirt road. The hike from here to Ka'ena Point is five miles round trip along the coast.

Another trail leads to Ka'ena Point from the other side of the Wai'anae mountain range, at Mokulē'ia. The trail is the only means of accessing the area; there is no road around this point.

Take water, sunscreen, and hats. Remember that this is a very remote area, and it is better to explore it in a group. Remember too that Ka'ena has some of the largest waves in Hawai'i, and in wintertime these blue mountains of water can reach heights of over forty feet. January/February is good for whale watching.

O'ahu

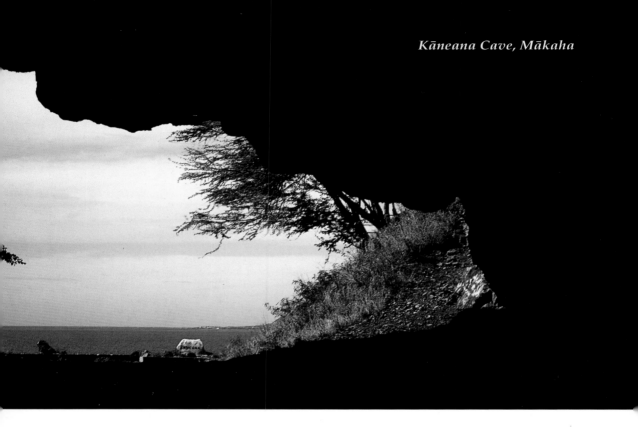

41. Kāneana Cave, Wai'anae District-
Home of the shark god's son

> *It led me downward,*
> *In the heart of the Wai'anae mountains,*
> *This cave of Mākua;*
> *It was dark, and damp, and very closed in,*
> *And I am sure I felt an evil force*
> *As if some dark, bloody deed had there been done;*
> *So strong was this sense of malevolency*
> *I hurried out*
> *Into the warm sunlight,*
> *Into the blinding day.*
> -Norah D. Stearns, Honolulu Star-Bulletin, 9 September 1939

GLOOMY KĀNEANA Cave was once a sea cave that was formed through the ages by the relentless power of the waves. At the entrance of the cave is a rock ledge, about twenty feet above the floor of the cave, that has wave-rounded boulders deposited by the sea thousands of years ago. The floor of the cave is beach sand covered by a black coating of particles that have dripped from the rocks through the long ages. The size of the cave is impressive; the entrance is over sixty feet high. The interior is huge and cavernous, and unfortunately it is now marked with graffiti. Dark, narrow passages lead to further caves, and black pits beckon the unwary. Take flashlights, and be careful where you step.

In ancient times, *kāhuna* conducted secret rituals here, and as recently as fifty years ago religious rites were performed here. In an old photograph, men can be seen standing within the cave's far depths, conducting rituals in the light of flaming *kukui* torches.

The cave is the ancient, legendary home of the shark god's son. This horrible personage could change from shark to man at will. As a handsome young man, he lured travelers into his cave then changed back into a shark and ate them on his slimy white stone altar at the back of the cave's watery depths. He was finally captured and killed by angry neighbors.
(Reference: Sterling and Summers 1978, 81.)

I wondered if people still remembered the story of the shark god's son. At the nearby beach park a Hawaiian man was playing a mellow tune on an 'ukulele. He said he knew of the shark god but that it was a very old story. The shark was his family 'aumakua, and he was never afraid in the ocean, as he knew the shark would protect him. When he went spear fishing, he always left some of his catch for the shark.

Directions: The cave is almost at the end of Farrington Highway as it winds along the beautiful, undeveloped Wai'anae Coast. The cave is just over three miles north of Mākaha Beach Park, next to the road on the *mauka* (mountain) side. There is a parking area opposite and a monument sign for Kāneana Cave.

War God Kū at Kāneʻākī Heiau

42. Kāneʻākī Heiau, Mākaha Valley, Waiʻanae District- *Restored war temple for Kū*

As GOD of war, Kū is prayed to as Kū the supreme one, Kū the snatcher of land, Kū the supporter, and Kū pulling together the earth. As god of sorcery, he is prayed to as Kū of the maggot-dropping mouth.

Kū, the war god of Kamehameha I, stands glaring above the altar of this *heiau*, waiting for what will come. This important *luakini heiau* has been perfectly reconstructed and resembles a functioning *heiau*, with thick black walls containing two main courtyards, a series of terraces leading to the altar, and tall oracle towers. Here *kāhuna* petitioned the gods while *aliʻi* waited for divine responses. The *hale mana* (house of spiritual power) and *hale pahu* (drum house) have been reconstructed. Behind the *heiau*, in the surrounding lush vegetation, is the platform that held the house of the *kāhuna*.

Kāneʻākī was originally an agricultural *heiau*, but when Kamehameha I decided to conquer Kauaʻi and quartered his army in Mākaha, his *kāhuna* advised using the *heiau* as a war temple to honor Kū.

The *heiau* stands in an Eden-like park. Peacocks run across the grass, little red birds sing and call out, tall yellow bamboo plants rustle, and *lilikoʻi* (passion fruit) lie on the ground. Once a *heiau* for human sacrifice, the temple now seems almost unreal and out of time and place. It's strange to think of the sacrifices made here; human sacrifices, their arms draped over pigs, were once placed on this altar. Even today the altar in front of Kū contains offerings, fortunately only of ti-leaf wrapped stones. (References: Beckwith 1970, 15; Sterling and Summers 1978, 77-78; Kamakau 1992, 44; Kirch 1985, 264, 265; Kirch 1996, 38-40.)

Thought to be Kūkā'ilimoku, idol carried into battle by Kamehameha the Great

Idols of the war god, Kū, now stand in the Bishop Museum. The idol that Kamehameha I carried into war, Kūkā'ilimoku, is approximately thirty inches tall. He has round, glaring, pearl-shell eyes, black feathered eyebrows and nostrils, and a snarling mouth filled with ninety-four dog teeth. The feathers on his head were said to bristle as he was carried into battle, and his wild screams rose above the sounds of the fighting (Kalākaua 1990, 18, 44).

Kū was the god of war, known for his desire for human sacrifice. He was introduced to Hawai'i by the kahuna Pā'ao, a powerful priest from Tahiti.

When the old gods were overthrown, Kū's keeper placed his image in a canoe and sent him out to sea, saying, "Here is your kapa, O Kū, here is your food. Go back to Kahiki."

Directions: Note that the *heiau* is only open from 10 a.m. to 2 p.m., Tuesday through Sunday; to make sure it is open, call Mauna'olu Estates Security at (808) 695-8174. Drive on the H1 Freeway to Mākaha and turn right at Mākaha Valley Road. The road goes up into the valley past the temporarily closed Sheraton Mākaha Hotel and the existing golf club. Follow the signs to the security gates of the Mauna'olu Estates, where you will need to show a driver's license and motor vehicle registration. Proceed straight ahead and follow signs for the *heiau*.

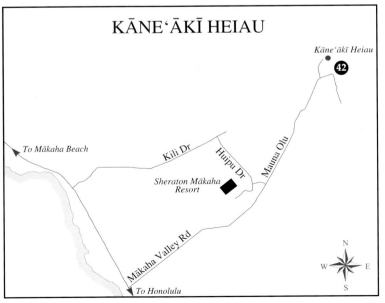

KĀNE'ĀKĪ HEIAU

Kāne'ākī Heiau

42

To Mākaha Beach

Kili Dr

Huipu Dr

Mauna Olu

Sheraton Mākaha Resort

Mākaha Valley Rd

To Honolulu

N
W E
S

Kūkaniloko Birthing Stones with offerings

43. Kūkaniloko, Wahiawā-
Birthplace of kapu chiefs

> *The time of the birth of the taboo chief,*
> *The time when the Heavenly One pushed his way out,*
> *The time when the bright one first saw the light,*
> *At first faintly like the light of the moon,*
> *At the season of Makali'i in the far past.*
> -from "Kumulipo," the Hawaiian creation chant
> (Beckwith 1972, 49)

HAPPY WAS the child born at Kūkaniloko, the sacred birthing stone! The child would be called a chief divine, a burning fire.

The ancient sacred stones are gathered together near the green pineapple fields of Wahiawā. The main stone, Kūkaniloko, is a large, brown lava rock with a sculptured area that supported the mother in a semi-sitting position while she gave birth. There are two high, pointed spots on each side of the stone, where chiefs or priests would sit to assist.

For the royal mother, giving birth was rather a public experience. Thirty-six chiefs, eighteen on each side, surrounded her. They came to witness the sacred birth and to give recognition to the bloodline and rank of mother, father, grandparents, and the newborn. The combined status of the parents determined the child's status.

The selection of the attendants and the way the mother was placed on the stone was governed by strict *kapu* rules. Adherence to the *kapu* ensured the full sanctity of birth at this powerful place. If the mother had complete trust in the site and was properly positioned, the child would be born with honor and the gods' blessings, and the mother would have an easy labor. A difficult delivery was a sign that the gods had not helped, and was viewed as a bad omen and a possible weakness in the bloodlines. Thousands of *maka'āinana* (commoners) would witness the birth from the far side of the stream. Torches flared and drums beat, resounding through the valley, announcing the birth of a great chief.

Chiefs born here enjoyed the distinction, privileges, and taboos not accorded to *ali'i* children born elsewhere. Mighty chiefs born at Kūkaniloko include Mā'ili-kūkahi, a great warrior; Kākuhihewa, an honored chief; and a female chief, Kūkaniloko, who was known for educating the young.

History records instances of chiefesses who went into labor and delivered their babies before reaching the birthstones. These children were considered "outside chiefs" and did not receive the special powers given those born at Kūkaniloko. Kamehameha I desired the full powers for his children and wanted his sacred wife, Keōpūolani, to give birth at the birthing stone, but she was unable to because of ill health.

Other ancient, weathered stones surround the birthing stone. Some were considered to possess powers of blessings; others were considered evil. Some stones were said to hold guardian spirits with the power to absorb pain.

The stones also had the reputation of being fertility stones; women would go here to pray to the gods for children, touch the stones, and make offerings. Many offerings are still seen at the stones today.
(References: Kamakau 1991, 38; Sterling and Summers 1978, 138-40; Ramirez 1998.)

Are the guardian spirits still at Kūkaniloko? Kalama, the Hawaiian kupuna who explained the significance of the stones to me, related how he had been restoring a broken stone when he had clearly seen the figure of a man leaving the stone. Kalama's ancestors were protectors of the stones, and his grandmother was born at this place.

"Did this give her extra prestige and powers?" I asked.

"Indeed, it did," he replied.

And then a strange thing happened. I began to feel deep pains. Maybe I was identifying with the mothers of the past. The last time I felt similar pains was when giving birth. This wasn't an experience I wanted to repeat, and I sat down on the grass and red dirt. Kalama asked me if I felt alright.

"Yes," I replied, not wanting to go into details before the tour guides and members of the Wahiawā Civic Club.

"Good," Kalama said, " Because often women who come to this site experience birthing pains."

Directions: Take Freeway H2 north to Wahiawā. Take the Wahiawā exit, Highway 80, which goes through the center of town. Past the town, turn left on Whitmore Avenue into a dirt road leading to a parking area. The birthing stones are in a grove of palm trees. From the parking area, it is a short walk to the stones.

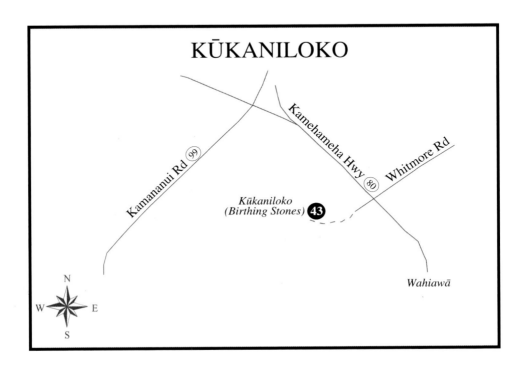

KŪKANILOKO

Kamananui Rd 99

Kamehameha Hwy 80

Whitmore Rd

Kūkaniloko
(Birthing Stones) **43**

Wahiawā

N
W E
S

43. Kūkauiloko, Wahiawā

*Healing Stone,
Pōhaku Hoʻola Kino*

44. Healing Stones of Wahiawā- *Healing for all*

BELIEF IN the healing powers of these stones has attracted visitors since ancient times. The two healing stones stand in a white tabernacle built in front of a residence on the suburban street of California Avenue in Wahiawā. The large, six-foot-tall black stone is called Pōhaku Hoʻola Kino (rock that gives health to the body). No one knows the name of the other stone.

The two stones were originally situated near the site of the birthing stones at Kūkaniloko. In 1927, workers from the pineapple fields began to visit the stones and soon reported miraculous cures. Crowds flocked to the stones, where people of different races prayed and left offerings.

It was feared that the crowds would damage the birthing stones, so the healing stones were moved to Wahiawā cemetery. Here they became even more popular, and the smaller stone became known for healing children.

In 1929, streams of pilgrims visited the stones from dawn to dusk. Chinese, Hawaiians, Koreans, Filipinos, and Japanese all prayed there. Leis were placed over the stones, incense filled the air, and stalls were erected to sell leis, bottles of water, incense, and fruit. Hindu worshipers considered the large stone to be a manifestation of the god Shiva, and they carved three grooves at the top of the stone to indicate this. As much as one thousand dollars a month was left in offerings. The money was used to improve the road and provide parking.

The Board of Health was called in, as some feared a health epidemic caused by the rotting food offerings. The stones were tested regularly for bacteria and disinfected twice a day, and a strict cleaning schedule was maintained.

When World War II broke out, gas shortages and curfews caused a decrease in the number of visitors to the stones. They were moved again and placed in a Japanese-shrine-like crypt at their present location on California Avenue in Wahiawā. Interest in the stones has died down, but there are still offerings at the altar. (References: Gutmanis 1977; Sterling and Summers 1978, 141.)

The tabernacle is directly in front of a house on California Avenue. When I visited the site the offertory box was filled with apples, oranges, a rotting banana, coins, and candy. Votive candles flicked before a statue of the Virgin Mary. A resident of the adjoining house was busy cleaning the shrine, scrubbing the marble, and wiping the altar.

"Do many people still come here for healing?" I asked.

"I don't know," he replied. "I don't know anything about the stones. They're in front of my house and I like to keep them clean."

Directions: Take H2 to the Wahiawā exit, Highway 80. Take a left turn at California Avenue and go past Kaʻala Elementary School on your right until you reach the intersection with Kaalalo Place. A Hawaiʻi Visitors Bureau sign and the shrine are on the right, next to the Olive United Methodist Church.

HEALING STONES

Kilani Ave

California St

Kaalalo

44 Healing Stones

Kamehameha Hwy

Wahiawā

H2

To Honolulu ▼

Ke-aīwa Heiau, 'Aiea, temple of healing

45. Keaīwa Heiau, 'Aiea-
Temple of healing

O Hina
I take the bark of this tree
For the purpose of curing the sickness of [name].
Undo all the troubles and afflictions,
And all the sickness upon his/her body.
And may this medicine become the healing
Medicine for him/her
O Hina.
-Hawaiian chant (Gutmanis 1977, 53)

SET AMONG beautiful trees and blessed with cool breezes, this *heiau* functioned as a healing or life-giving *heiau*. Only a small part of the original temple is left. The thick walls are of a double-wall construction to withstand earthquakes. A large *hālau* (thatched-roof house) probably stood in the middle of the walls; the home of the *kāhuna lapaʻau*, his workshop, classroom, and operating room. Images of the gods from whom he sought help surrounded him, among them perhaps Lono and the goddess Hina.

Patients were often treated with steam baths in a *hau* tree hut built over a pit. Water was poured over hot stones in the pit to create steam. It was *kapu* for women to enter the *heiau*, so they were treated in their own house outside.

Young people were brought to Keaīwa to be trained as healing priests. Training began from the age of five, and the instruction was comprehensive. The venerated *kāhuna* were experts in the arts of healing and had a vast knowledge of medicinal plants. They used herbs and prayers to heal the sick and were adept at handling common health problems. A great herb garden lay outside the *heiau* walls, and the *kāhuna* also collected plants from the mountains. Specimens of some plants used are still growing around the *heiau*. The name Keaīwa means "the mysterious," and it refers to the mysterious healing powers of the *kāhuna*.

This is still considered a temple of healing today. There were offerings of ti-leaf wrapped stones and fruit on the *heiau* when we visited, and incense sticks had been inserted in the rocks. A group of seven people, draped in blue gowns and led by a white-clad *kahuna*, chanted for over an hour at the altar. They told us that they were on a tour of healing places on the islands and that this place had a special energy.
(Reference: Sterling and Summers 1978, 11-12.)

Today in Honolulu, native Hawaiian healers work with physicians to promote healing. On July 14, 1998, Governor Ben Cayetano signed into law a bill allowing Hawaiian healers to offer their skills as licensed practitioners. This led to Papa Henry Auwae's practicing alternate healing techniques side by side with Dr. Emmett Aluli and Dr. Phillip Reyes at Molokaʻi's General Hospital in Kaunakakai.
(Reference: Creamer 1998.)

In Honolulu we visited Francine Dudoit, a registered nurse who practices Hawaiian healing in her clinic at 333 North King Street. Francine has a calm and caring aura around her, and I had to restrain myself from relating medical problems-my own, my friends', and my family's. She

45. Keaīwa Heiau

inspired that kind of confidence. Instead we spoke about the noni plant. Francine says that this is an absolute miracle plant. We tasted some of the cool, pleasant-tasting, slightly fizzy liquid drained from the fermented noni fruit. Francine has found small doses of noni extremely effective in treating diabetic patients who cannot use insulin, and it has also been effective in treating lupus, high cholesterol, glaucoma, gum infections, and boils. Scientists have recently discovered that the juice contains xeronine, an alkaloid, and noni is used in medicines for tuberculosis. Francine harvests the fruit from her farm on Moloka'i and sends sealed containers to patients on the islands and overseas. Noni apparently purifies the blood. The plant was respected by the healers of old-there is almost always a noni tree to be found in the vicinity of a heiau.

Francine related that one of the most amazing effects she has seen the noni plant bring about was the reconstruction of the foot of a diabetic patient. Medical practitioners had wanted to amputate the foot, but application of noni pulp dressings completely restored it. Her clinic works on patients' diets, gives lomilomi (massage), and regards the spiritual aspect of healing as most important.

The Dudoit family came from a long line of kāhuna, originally from the great healing kāhuna of Moloka'i. Some of the kāhuna in the family, however, were kāhuna 'anā'anā-the sorcerers of Moloka'i, and they were very powerful too! Francine can be reached at her clinic-call (808) 922-3776.

In 1998 the German pharmaceutical giant Schwabe had a representative looking for sources of 'awa on Moloka'i. This plant is also known as kava kava. It has been used for generations in the Pacific as a drink featured in cultural ceremonies. Its health claims include treatment of depression and hyperactivity. It seems quite effective; most people drinking kava at ceremonies in the Pacific have a very mellow look! But beware, you may run the risk of becoming like Chief Kalaniʻōpuʻu, "palsied by a lifetime of ʻawa drinking."

Directions: Take the H1 Freeway heading ʻewa (westward). Do not take the H1 fork to the right, but proceed straight ahead on Highway 78, past the stadium and Hālawa exits, and take the ʻAiea exit. Follow this exit to ʻAiea Heights Drive, and turn right up the hill. At the end of the road is Heaīwa State Recreation Area (open 7 a.m. to 6:30 p.m.). The *heiau* is at the entrance to the park. There is a scenic 4.5-mile-round-trip hike in the park. Follow the park road to the ʻAiea Loop Trail, which leads through pine and eucalyptus forests. In season, the red cherry guavas are delicious and a good source of vitamin C.

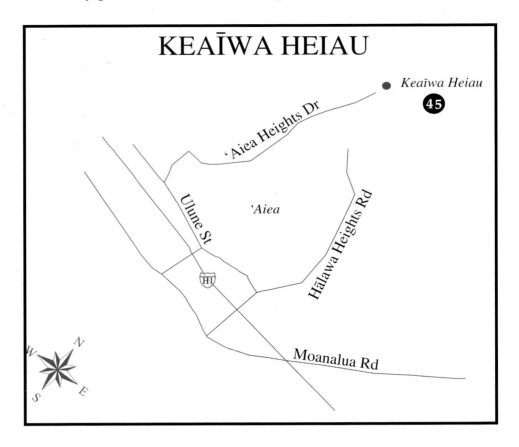

KEAĪWA HEIAU

Keaīwa Heiau

45

ʻAiea Heights Dr

ʻAiea

Ulune St

Hālawa Heights Rd

H1

Moanalua Rd

45. Keaīwa Heiau

Pūowaina, Punchbowl Crater, hill of sacrifice

46. Pūowaina, Punchbowl- *Hill of sacrifice*

IN PROUD remembrance of the achievements of her sons and in humble tribute to their sacrifices this memorial has been erected by the United States of America
1941-1945 1950-1953 1961-1973
-inscription on the chapel vestibule at Punchbowl

Pūowaina (Hill of Sacrifice) is the ancient Hawaiian name for Punchbowl Crater. The name was prophetic. Punchbowl Crater, green and peaceful as it rises from the heart of Honolulu, holds the bodies of almost twenty-five thousand men and women who fought for the United States from the time of the Spanish-American War to that of the Vietnam War.

The ancient Hawaiian people held the crater as consecrated ground and an important place of sacrifice. When people broke the *kapu*, the whole island was placed in jeopardy. The punishments of the gods were fearsome: earthquakes, hot volcanic lava, devastating tidal waves. Sacrifices were considered necessary to placate the hungry gods. On this hill of sacrifice, there was a fire oven that was used for burning the bodies of defeated chiefs and warriors and people who had violated the *kapu* system of the great chiefs. The oven was said to have a good updraft for the fires.

Breakers of the *kapu* were drowned at a spring near Kewalo Street. Their cooperation was expected; the priests wanted an unblemished sacrifice. "Lie quietly in the arms of your chief," they would tell the unlucky victim. If the victim resisted, family members would be sacrificed. The body would be carried in a solemn procession by *kāhuna* who made an awesome sight with their flowing white garments exposing one arm and shoulder and the white *malo* around their loins. Bands of white *kapa* were wrapped around their heads. The victim's body was placed on the large stone altar. This altar stone has now been excavated to make way for the concrete overlook on the crater's rim. A human sacrifice occurred here as late as 1809.

From this fearsome past, Punchbowl Crater emerged as one of the world's greatest tributes to selfless sacrifice. Thousands of granite markers tell of the sacrifices and deaths of the war heroes buried here. Nearly 2.6 million people visit to pay tribute each year. They walk slowly through the Courts of the Missing, where marble slabs list the names of more than twenty thousand MIAs, whose bodies were never found. They admire the huge, colorful battle maps listing names of places that still resound in our memories: Pearl Harbor, Wake, Midway, Iwo Jima, Coral Sea, Gilbert Islands, Okinawa. Many of Hawai'i's war dead were of Japanese ancestry. The visitors stand in awe and silence in the beautiful memorial chapel. They walk to the grave of Ernie Pyle, the famous and loved war correspondent. They remember those who gave their lives and made the ultimate sacrifice, and they grieve. A visit to Punchbowl Crater is a moving experience.
(References: Carlson 1992; Sterling and Summers 1978, 291, 292.)

The crater holds a strategic position high over Honolulu. It played a part in the bloody battle when Kamehameha I conquered the ruler of O'ahu. The O'ahu warriors fled through the crater and met their deaths on the cliffs of the Pali.

In 1816 eight heavy guns were placed on Pūowaina as a precaution against a Russian invasion. In 1895 the guns were fired in anger to thwart an attempt to restore the monarchy during a conflict between the Royalist supporters and the supporters of a Hawaiian republic. The

46. Pūowaina, Punchbowl

queen's guards led a contingent against the small force of republicans at Pūowaina. Fifteen shells were fired, threatening the queen's guards with annihilation. They surrendered.

When World War II broke out in the Pacific, local defense forces decided to use Punchbowl Crater as a site for its gun emplacements to defend the island from a possible attack. Ironically, it was presumed that the attack would come from the sea. Thus the battery on Punchbowl would have been ineffective against an air attack.

As the terrible war continued, thousands died in the Pacific. Bodies were brought to Honolulu and kept in mausoleum warehouses. In 1949 the first burial service took place at Punchbowl, and "Taps" echoed hauntingly across the crater.

Directions: On the H1 Freeway traveling west, take the Lunalilo exit, proceed two blocks to Pensacola Avenue, and turn right. Proceed until it becomes Auwaiolimu Street, passing Roosevelt High School and Lincoln Elementary School, until you reach Pūowaina Drive. Turn left and follow the sign to Punchbowl National Cemetery of the Pacific at 2177 Pūowaina Drive.

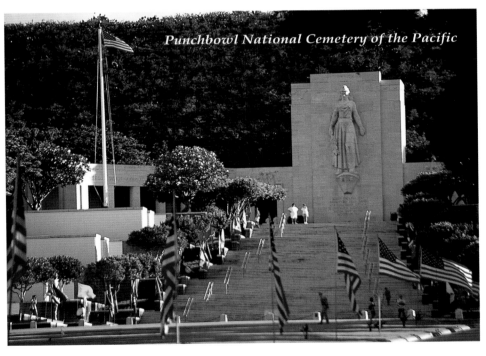

Punchbowl National Cemetery of the Pacific

Wizard Stones named after four wizards from Tahiti who came to O'ahu and taught healing.

47. Wizard Stones of Waikīkī-
Place of healing

THESE FOUR large ancient stones are said to contain the *mana* of four wizards who came to O'ahu from Tahiti many years ago. Although tall and manly, the wizards were feminine in their habits. Some called them "unsexed." It is said that the rocks indicate the hermaphrodite nature of the wizards.

The wizards settled near where the Moana Surfrider Hotel is today, and they cured the ill by laying on of hands. They also taught healing skills.

Before the wizards left, they gave instructions that the stones be placed at the beach in memory of their visit. Thousands of Hawaiians moved the four huge black stones from Kaimukī to Waikīkī. After the stones were placed, the people celebrated and feasted, and the wizards performed healing rituals for one more month. They told the people that they were leaving their power in the stones and then sailed off, never to return.

Princess Likelike used to place a lei on each of the stones before swimming at Waikīkī.
(Reference: Pukui, Haertig, and Lee 1972, 2: 108.)

Do these stones possess healing power? Is the mana of the wizards in the rocks? Some believe that it is.

We spoke to an elderly man who was chatting with his friends on the benches near the stones. He said that he was very annoyed that a fence had been built around the stones, as it made it difficult for people to get near them.

Directions: The stones are at the Kūhiō Beach Park on Kalākaua Avenue in Waikīkī, near the police substation.

Classic image of surfing in Waikīkī with exotic Diamond Head as a backdrop

Two ferocious lion statues guard the entrance to Mānoa Chinese Cemetery

48. Mānoa Chinese Cemetery-
Home of fireballs and spirits

You take care of the dead, and they'll take care of you.
-caretaker, Mānoa Chinese Cemetery (Grant 1996)

IN ANCIENt Hawai'i, Mānoa Valley was considered a place full of
mana. There were many *heiau*, including an owl *heiau*, and secret
burial caves.

Mānoa Chinese Cemetery, occupying a prime position in
the valley, has a reputation of being haunted and is also well
known for sightings of fireballs. Over many years, tales have
spread about the glowing fires and swirling little balls of light that
fly over the graves here. A belief in ghost lights is found in many
cultures. Some believe that fireballs are the spirits of human souls
tormented with jealousy, hatred, revenge, or love. The Hawaiians
refer to fireballs as *akua lele*, or flying gods, usually poison gods
sent to destroy. Some say that the appearance of such a ball of light
is an omen of impending death.

I visited the cemetery to see these fireballs. The night was dark, and some from the tour group stumbled as they approached the graves. There had been an inauspicious beginning to the Ghost Tour. One member of the group, a slim attractive woman, had collapsed at my feet as we waited for the bus. We'd waited for the ambulance and watched as she was carried off on a stretcher. Then the bus roared through the dark, foggy streets of Mānoa to the cemetery. I, too, now felt rather shaky.

We were taken to a particularly heart-rending section of the graveyard, the children's section. Here, young children are buried together so that they may play with one another. A schoolteacher's grave lies up the slope from the graves of the children. Legend says that her eyes gleam from the grave at night. We looked intently past the little white headstones of the children's graves to the teacher's grave. Certainly something was gleaming. One wouldn't want to investigate too closely; it's unlucky and disrespectful to go tramping over graves.

Ancient Hawaiians regarded Mānoa Valley as a sacred place. Legend says they showed it to the Chinese astronomer Lum Chang in 1852, when he was searching for a special place for a Chinese cemetery. Lum Chang was immediately drawn to the valley.

"We are at an extraordinary spot," he told his companion as they climbed to the top of the peculiar knoll in the center of the valley. "This place is the pulse of the watchful dragon of the valley. People from all directions will come from across the seas and gather here to pay homage. Birds, too, will come to sing and roost. It is a haven suitable for the living as well as the dead. The Chinese people must buy this area and keep it as sacred ground."

Lum Chang was highly respected by the Chinese community living in Hawai'i in 1852. He was a master of geomancy, the art of divination. Using his "magic instruments" and his knowledge of astronomy and geology, he had correlated the stars to the geographic features of the earth, and all the necessary elements combined in Mānoa Valley. The Chinese community did indeed buy the "dragon's pulse," and it is now the Mānoa Chinese Cemetery. Chinese ancestor worship assumes that the dead have the same "senses" as the living and enjoy the pleasant surroundings, misty rains, and rainbows of the valley. Other needs of ancestors are also catered for, and in the graveyard one sees food and fruit left for the dead, even cigarettes left for a beloved grandfather. (Reference: Thom 1985.)

Directions: Take University Avenue toward the mountains, and turn right at the traffic light at East Mānoa Road. Proceed about 1.5 miles to the end of the valley at Pakanu St. Straight ahead you will see the entrance to the cemetery, guarded by two ferocious lion statues. The beautiful mountains behind the cemetery can be accessed via the exotic Lyon Arboretum at the end of nearby Mānoa Road.

Lion and elephant statues guard the pavilion stairs

Mānoa chinese Cemetery

Pōhakuloa Stone, where women prayed for healthy and wise children

49. Pōhakuloa Stone, Punahou-
Stone that gives wisdom

Pregnant women and infertile women once bowed down and prayed to this six-foot-high "long stone" hoping for healthy, wise children. Appropriately, it now stands at the gates of Punahou School, a place where children can acquire wisdom.

The Punahou stone was part of a very large boulder, possibly a birthing stone, that stood on the northeastern slope of Mānoa hill. The stone was declared *kapu* when it apparently refused to be moved. Workmen, attempting to move the stone, noted that each morning it had burrowed itself deeper into the ground. A *kahuna* advised the workmen that the stone had a spirit, and it would only move if coaxed to do so. They prepared and ate a great feast of chicken, fish, pig, and poi before the stone. After the feast, the digging began again and the stone, held upright by two men, moved of its own accord.

Interestingly, another stone from the same boulder was placed at a location that would later become the site of the

Kapi'olani Hospital for Women and Children, perhaps another example of the *mana* of the stone.

In the 1830s hundreds of prisoners convicted of adultery were placed in a prison gang to build the wall surrounding the Punahou acreage and the house of Reverend Bingham. Hawaiians, who regarded the sex act and coital excellence as the greatest gifts the gods could bestow, deeply resented the new edict against adultery. King Kamehameha III decided that if his people were guilty of adultery, he was himself just as guilty, and joined the wall builders in sympathy. The Hawaiian people loved him for his humble act.

(Reference: Sterling and Summers 1978, 283.)

Directions: The stone is located at the Punahou Street entrance gate of Punahou School, at the corner of Wilder Street and Punahou Street in Honolulu.

Hanauma Bay, where royalty relaxed

50. Hanauma Bay and Kohelepelepe, East Honolulu-
The traveling vagina

> *Little fish with wicked eye;*
> *Snub-nosed fish that swims the deep;*
> *Sworded fish that dots and stabs*
> *Among the blue sea coral groves-*
> *Alas, the shark has done for me,*
> *The mighty shark, mine enemy!*
> -Hawaiian chant (Emerson 1978, 71)

Hanauma Bay is a beautiful little cove, actually the sea-eroded crater of an extinct volcano. A reef protects the bay, and thousands of brightly-colored tropical fish cruise the maze of underwater lava channels. The name Hanauma means "a curved bay," or "hand-wrestling bay," and the *ali'i* played the game of *uma* (hand-

wrestling) here on long summer after-
noons. Queen Kaʻahumanu came here
by canoe and swam in the crystal waters, and the bay was a favorite fishing
spot of Kamehameha V.

O Jisan, shrine to a Japanese guardian spirit, next to Hālona Blowhole

There were many fish shrines
along this coast. A shrine to a visiting god
stands on a nearby cliff overlooking the
rock shelf at Hālona Blowhole. Built by
the Honolulu Japanese Casting Club, O
Jisan, a Japanese guardian spirit of protection, is carved into the large rock monument to keep watch over anglers. When
we visited, the shrine was covered with
coins, and a cream satin bow from a
wedding dress lay at O Jisan's feet.

Nearby Koko Crater, a botanical
garden, was the scene of a strange event. According to legend, the
swinish pig-god Kamapuaʻa pursued Pele here with the intention
of raping her. Luckily her sister Kapo, with great presence of
mind, flung her magical *kohe lele* (traveling vagina) to distract
Kamapuaʻa. It left its imprint on the hill, known thereafter as
Kohelepelepe, and then flew off to Kalihi.

*Swimming at Hanauma Bay, in clouds of shining fish, is a magical
experience. Early morning is the best time to visit. We walked over the
lava rocks and tide pools to the left of the bay and came to the "Toilet
Bowl." Waves were foaming into an exposed lava tube, sucking four
screaming swimmers to the bottom of the bubbling, churning pool and
then flinging them up and out. Will jumped in and whooped as the surge
carried him up and over the brim. A happy exhibitionist dove into a
smaller hole, swam through the tube, and emerged in the large pool,
challenging fate, as a number of swimmers have drowned by getting
jammed in the crevices. A girl tried frantically to climb out, sliding back
down into the pool each time the waves ebbed, and clutching sections of
her bikini, which she was in dire danger of losing. There's always something happening in Hawaiʻi!*

50. Hanauma Bay and Kohelepelepe

Directions: Follow Kalaniana'ole Highway east to Koko Marina Shopping Center, where you can pick up a picnic at Subway before heading uphill to Hanauma Bay. The "Toilet Bowl" is a short walk around the rock ledges to the left of the cove. Keep an eye out for waves that sometimes sweep over the rocks.

From Hanauma Bay, drive about four hundred yards to the O Jisan shrine and Hālona Blowhole. Pretty Eternity Beach, adjacent to the Blowhole, was featured in the love scene in the film "From Here to Eternity." Locals sometimes call it Maternity Beach-nevertheless, it provides safe and fun swimming!

A mile farther along is Sandy Beach, with cute beachgoers and impressive surfers but some nasty shore breaks. Turn left at the traffic lights on Kealahou Street and three hundred yards later on your left you'll come to the turnoff for Koko Head Crater (Kohelepelepe) and Botanic Gardens, which provides a pleasant late afternoon hike through succulents and an arid landscape.

Kohelepelepe or Koko Head Crater, scene of a very strange event which left its imprint in shaping the hill

51. Ulupō Heiau, Kailua-
Temple with a menehune pathway

> *O the four hundred gods*
> *The four thousand gods*
> *The four hundred thousand gods*
> *The assembly of gods*
> *The rows of gods*
> *The groups of gods*
> *O come! Here is work*
> -"Chant to avoid insulting or overlooking any gods"
> (Luomala 1986, 135)

A SINISTER brooding giant, this massive *heiau* of ancient lava rock, measuring 140 by 180 feet with walls up to 30 feet in height, lies hidden on the slopes of Ka-wai-nui Marsh in suburban Kailua. The name Ulupō means "Night Inspiration."

Ulupō is so ancient that it is believed the *menehune* built it. The small *menehune* had a reputation for hard work, and they are believed to have hauled the rocks a long distance, passing them down a line hand-to-hand in a single night. A pathway of stones leading across the platform is known as the "*Menehune* Pathway."

At the base of the huge northwest wall is a small freshwater spring where sacrifices for the *heiau* were first washed. Originally this was an agricultural *heiau*, and the area under the shady trees is filled with taro, banana trees, and *ti* plants. The *heiau* was later made into a *luakini heiau*, and Kamehameha I's warriors are said to have dragged the defeated warriors of O'ahu up these narrow paths and sacrificed them on the altar.

Several O'ahu chiefs, along with their families and attendants, lived in the fertile Kailua Valley and participated at ceremonies here. The fierce tattooed Maui chief Kahekili, after conquering the O'ahu high chief Kahahana in the 1780s, lived in the vicinity of the *heiau* and took part in rituals.

The O'ahu warriors resented their conquerors, and history records that a group of eight warriors, filled with valor and a total disregard of consequences, decided to inflict as much damage as they could on the invaders. The eight men boldly charged a contingent of several hundred men and, using their spears and javelins with amazing skill, killed many of their enemies. As the eight men were endeavoring to escape, Chief Ka-uhi-ko'ako'a captured Maka'i-o-ulu, a good fighter but a bad runner because of his short bowlegs. The Maui chief swung his captive onto his back and ran off, intending to sacrifice him. Maka'i-o-ulu, wishing to avoid a slow, painful death, called out to his friend Pupuka to throw a spear through his navel and kill him. Pupuka threw the spear, Maka'i-o-ulu dodged violently to the side, and the spear went through Chief Ka-uhi-ko'ako'a's back. Seeing their leader fall, the Maui warriors gave up the pursuit, and the eight gallant warriors escaped.

The structures on the *heiau* included an altar, a twenty-foot-high oracle tower for communing with the gods, thatched houses to store the ceremonial drums and sacred water, an oven, and ferocious wooden images of the gods.

Symbolic sacrifices still appear here today. Rocks or bananas are carefully wrapped in the leaves of the sacred *ti* plant, and leis of plumeria flowers lie on the lichen-covered rocks.

(References: Sterling and Summers 1978, 233; Kamakau 1992, 135.)

The guide for Hawai'i Ghost Tours gave each of us a ti leaf for protection and sprinkled us with salt; then we cautiously stumbled down the dark path leading to Ulupō heiau. It was a moonless night, and the heiau looked very black and forbidding. The swamp around it was very silent. I wanted to walk up the pathway leading to the top of the heiau and look over the eerie landscape, but the guide advised strongly against it.

He said that on a previous tour a young woman had climbed the heiau, kicked the stones, and called it "a big pile of rocks." Her three colleagues and the other tour members had been upset and felt that spirits would follow her and the tour would be doomed.

The following day, the young woman's colleagues contacted the guide to tell him that the young woman had awakened with legs that were red, puffy, and swollen to three times their normal size. They had taken her to a kahuna who said a blessing, and she went back to the heiau, left an offering, and apologized. Her legs returned to normal size.

Directions: Proceed toward Kailua on Highway 61. About two blocks past the intersection with Kalaniana'ole Highway (Castle Hospital is at the intersection), turn left on Uluoa Street and then right on Manu Aloha Street. Park at the YMCA building and walk around the gate, following the Hawai'i Visitors Bureau sign to the heiau.

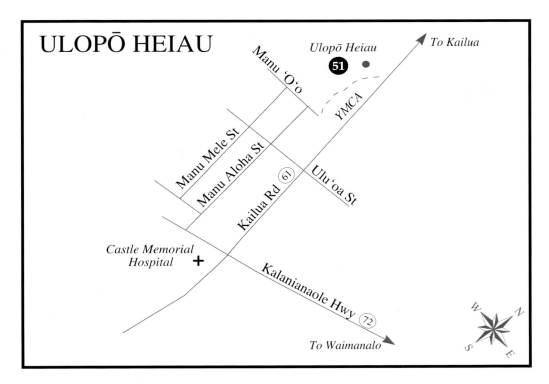

51. Ulupō Heiau

John Morgan on horseback at Kualoa Ranch

52. Kualoa Valley, North Kāne'ohe Bay- *Secret burial caves and night marchers*

To the Chief belongs the whole land,
To the Chief belongs the ocean and the land;
The night is his; the day is his;
For him are the seasons, the winter, the summer,
The month, the seven stars of heaven now risen,
The property of the Chiefs, above and below,
All things that float ashore, the bird driven upon the land,
The thick-shelled, broad-backed turtle, the dead whale is cut up;
The yearly uhu of the sea,
Let the Chief live forever! Evermore a Chief!
Let him be borne forth gloriously with the short gods and the
long gods.
Let him go forth fearlessly, the Chief holding the island.
-from the "Haui ka Lani" canto foretelling the ascendancy
of Kamehameha I (Handy et al. 1965, 187)

EMERALD GREEN Kualoa Valley was declared by the high priest Kaopulupulu to be one of the most sacred places on the island of O'ahu. Pohukaina, O'ahu's most famous burial cave for chiefs, is in the mountains overlooking the valley. Tradition says that the cave is full of treasures: sacred ivory, carved idols, and red-and-yellow-feathered capes are said to be hidden in its secret caverns amid dark rivers and streams.

The cherished newborn children of the chiefs were brought to this *kapu* area and lived here with their foster parents. They were trained in the arts of war and ancient traditions. The royal *kapa* of their fathers blew in the wind. When fishermen passed, they had to lower their sails; breaking of this *kapu* meant death to the fishermen. Victims for sacrificial ceremonies on the *luakini heiau* were drowned in the tranquil blue ocean here and called *ka limu o Kawahine*, the seaweed of *Kawahine*.

Kualoa was so sacred that it also held a place of refuge, where breakers of the *kapu* and defeated warriors could flee. If they succeeded in entering the place of refuge, the *kāhuna* would provide shelter, protection, and forgiveness, which would permit the former *kapu* breaker to reenter the community in safety.

Around 1775 Kahahana, a young chief, became ruler of the land. His wily uncle, the great tattooed chief of Maui, Kahekili, asked for the wealthy area of Kualoa as a reward for having raised Kahahana. The young chief was agreeable to this proposal, but fortunately he consulted a *kahuna*, who warned him, "O chief! If you give away these things your authority will be lost, and you will cease to be a ruler. To Kualoa belong the watercourses of your ancestors, the sacred drums. Without the ivory that drifts ashore, you could not offer to the gods the first victim slain in battle; it would be for Kahekili to offer it on Maui, and the rule would become his. You would no longer be ruler . . . and be sure not to conceal from me any further secret message that Kahekili may send."

Kahahana and his counselors congratulated themselves upon their escape from losing dominion to Kahekili. It was not long, however, before the great schemer Kahekili poisoned Kahahana's mind against his faithful *kahuna*. Kahahana treacherously murdered both the *kahuna* and his son. Kahekili, having removed his main opposition, then invaded O'ahu and routed Kahahana's warriors, and Kualoa became his.

52. Kualoa Valley

The sorceress Pahulu (see Site 30) from Lānaʻi is said to have lived at Kualoa, and the remains of her *heiau* are said to be on land jutting into the ocean across from the old sugar mill. (References: Kamakau 1992, 129-38; Sterling and Summers 1978, 176-78.)

Koʻolau Mountains tower over the ranch

Kualoa has a pleasant camping ground, but take care! In the evening, mists over the towering mountains form godlike shapes and people report hearing drums on dark nights sacred to the god Kāne. Some have seen night marchers here-chiefs and warriors in huge ghostly processions, marching from their burial caves high in the mountains to the sea. Some of the many road accidents in the area have been attributed to these sightings.

The beautiful Kualoa Ranch sprawls at the foot of the fluted green pali (cliffs). The Morgan family, descendants of the great missionary Dr. G. P. Judd, have ownership interest in and manage the ranch. Their recollections of unusual events that have occurred here are fascinating.

Margo Morgan heard the beating of the ancient drums sounding through the isolated gullies, and on one memorable evening her entire dinner party of guests heard them too.

Similarly, one night her niece, driving the dark, winding road over the Pali, slammed on her brakes and brought her car to a sudden halt.

"What are you doing?" her passenger shouted.

"Didn't you see them?" she asked." Didn't you see the night marchers crossing the road right in front of us?"

John Morgan knows of no verifiable sightings of night marchers. He does, however, practice caution. When his Hawaiian building contractor advised him that he was building his new home right in the path of night marchers, he agreed to relocate the building site.

The remains of more than four hundred chiefs are said to be buried in the caves above Kualoa Ranch. A stream that flowed out of a hole in the cliffs (now buried under the rubble from military bunkers built into the hillside) was said to be connected to an underground river running through Pohukaina Cave, which led all the way to 'Iolani Palace. Francis Morgan often rode his horse in this area, and the horse normally stopped to drink from the stream. One day, however, the horse reared and refused to go anywhere near the stream. Francis had to return home. The following day, he passed the stream again and saw an offering there. He asked a Hawaiian paniolo (cowboy) at the ranch what the offering meant.

"The akua (gods) came out yesterday to have a look around," the cowboy replied. "The offering is for them."

Directions: Take Kahekili Highway (85) north from Kāne'ohe. You are getting close to Kualoa Regional Park when you see Chinaman's Hat (the little island in the shape of a hat) offshore. Kualoa Ranch is across the road from the park entrance, eighty yards farther north, and it is a beautiful place to visit. The ranch has horse trails that wind into the sacred mountains. For activity and trail ride reservations, call (808) 237-7321. The ranch has museum exhibits and a replica Hawaiian village with hands-on experience of Hawaiian games such as spear throwing. John Morgan is planning an *ahupua'a,* **a fully self-supporting land district from mountain to sea, at Mōli'i Fishpond.**

At left; Chinaman's Hat, Kualoa, the remains of a mighty dragon lizard.
Below; Mōli'i Fishpond,

52. Kualoa Valley

53. Pu'uomahuka Heiau, Pūpūkea-
Where British sailors met their doom

> *Ye gods that smack your lips,*
> *Ye gods that whisper,*
> *Ye gods that watch by night*
> *Ye gods that show your gleaming eyes by night*
> *Come down, awake, make a move, stir yourselves,*
> *Here is your food, a house.*
> -Hawaiian chant, "Undying Power of the Gods"
> (Gutmanis 1983, 13)

BUILD HIGH and the gods will hear you! This is what the *kāhuna* believed when they recommended the building of Pu'uomahuka Heiau. This *heiau*, the largest on O'ahu, stands on a bluff in a commanding position. The view is panoramic, overlooking Waimea Bay-one of the world's top surfing beaches-lush green fields, and peaceful Waimea Stream.

This was a *luakini heiau*, built by a warrior king to honor the war god, Kū, and to pray for success in battle. Oʻahu's chief wished to know if Kauaʻi's warriors would surrender to his war canoes. The temple was built high on the cliffs, so the *kāhuna* could stand at the twenty-foot-high oracle tower and be close to the gods as they asked this important question. The first *heiau* in the area had been built near the beach, and the *kāhuna* had been unable to contact the gods from its low position.

The original temple on the bluff was so ancient that historians believe *menehune* built it. The larger temple, built in the twelfth century, was placed on its original foundations and required an enormous amount of hard work. Commoners had to leave their taro fields and assist in the building. People seeking the advice of the *kāhuna* had to carry stones up the hill; the larger the favor, the greater the stone.

At the dedication of the temple, the bodies of victims who had broken the *kapu* were laid on the altar and burned. The fires from the numerous sacrifices were so large that the glow could be seen on Kauaʻi, one hundred miles away. The sacred drums could be heard across the valley.

The war god, Kū, was not choosy about his sacrifices; a few British sailors joined the list of victims. In 1793 Vancouver's ship, the Daedalus, anchored in this peaceful-looking bay. Three English sailors went ashore to get water for the ship from the stream and were watched silently from above by warriors from the *heiau*. These were fearsome warriors, loyal to the conquering Maui chief, Kahekili, and tattooed completely over half of their bodies, including the insides of their eyelids. They noted the sailors' weapons and liked what they saw. Pouring down the cliffs, they captured and killed the sailors and sacrificed their bodies on the altar.

This *heiau* was a powerful place, and *aliʻi* regarded it as a very desirable place to be born. The rocky crevices and nooks became a maternity hospital with a panoramic view. *Piko* were placed in the crevices of boulders.

Kamehameha the Great worshiped here after he conquered Oʻahu in 1797. His important high priest, Hewahewa, officiated at rituals. Later, Hewahewa foretold the coming of the missionaries to their exact landing point. He foresaw that their powers would be stronger than his and, losing faith in his own gods, he was instru-

53. Puʻuomahuka Heiau

mental in ordering the destruction of *heiau* throughout the islands. Hewahewa became one of the first Christians in Hawai'i at nearby Lili'uokalani Protestant Church in Hale'iwa. He is buried at Waimea Falls Park.

Secret rituals are still performed today at isolated sacred sites in Hawai'i. Here, the *lele* altar has been restored and overflows with offerings of flower leis, apples, papaya, pineapples, and stones wrapped in *ti* leaves. The old gods are not forgotten.
(Reference: Sterling and Summers 1978, 142-44.)

The small Church of Hawai'i Nei is at the bottom corner of Pūpūkea Road, as it meets Kamehameha Highway. There we met Mama Loa, a wonderfully articulate Hawaiian lady with a flower-bedecked hat and kukui bead necklaces. Mama Loa told us she helped restore the altar of the heiau and was helping restore the ancient Hawaiian faith.

"I was born on the Big Island, and my mother taught me to pray in honor of Tutu Pele, the goddess of fire," she said. "My father dedicated me to Tutu Pele at the crater. My parents also taught me to pray to Jesus and to share the love of God."

"To whom are the offerings on this altar made?" we asked.

"To Tutu Pele," she replied.

Intrigued by the apparent merger of world views, we asked, "What is the relationship between Tutu Pele and Jesus?"

"Jesus recognizes Tutu Pele as a powerful god," Mama Loa solemnly replied. "God bless you and give you lots of aloha." She smiled serenely at us.

Directions: From Hale'iwa, follow Kamehameha Highway past Waimea Bay. Turn mauka (toward the mountains) at Foodland on Pūpūkea Road. The road winds up the hill. After two hundred yards, a turnoff to the right, marked with a visitor's sign, leads about a mile along a road to the *heiau*.

Waimea Bay is a world-famous surfing beach where in winter surfers ride monstrous twenty-five-foot-high waves. Watching them is amazing. The valley was a sacred site and holds a number of *heiau*. Waimea Falls Park is an extremely scenic tourist attraction. At its entrance is Hale o Lono, a restored he*iau* with replicas of a *mana* house, oracle tower, drum house, and image of Lono. There is also a pit containing the partial remains of a human sacrifice. Although there is a fee to enter Waimea Falls Park, no admission fee is required to visit the *heiau*.

Before you leave beautiful Waimea Bay, stop for a minute and pay a silent tribute to Eddie Aikau. Eddie was the first lifeguard here, and he is respected for the many lives he saved in the monster waves and for the surfing competitions he won. He stunned the crowds on the beach when he rode a giant forty-foot wave set, beautifully merging with the power of the ocean.

In 1978, when the Hōkūleʻa set out to sail to Tahiti, Eddie was among the crew. The sixty-foot double-hulled canoe overturned in heavy weather in one of the most treacherous stretches of ocean on earth. Taking on water, lashed by gale force winds, and pounded by twelve-foot swells, the canoe drifted out of shipping lanes and away from potential rescue. Hope seemed to be fading for the crew members clinging to the hull. Eddie decided to

53. *Puʻuomahuka Heiau*

View from Pu'uomahuka Heiau of Waimea Bay

paddle his board for Lāna'i, some twelve miles to the east. A strong, fearless swimmer, Eddie went for help. He set off through the giant swells, and he was never seen again.

Eddie is a true Hawaiian hero. When the waves reach heights of over twenty feet, the Quiksilver in Memory of Eddie Aikau Big Wave Invitational is held at Waimea Bay.

A popular bumper sticker on cars in Hawai'i carries the words "Eddie Would Go."
(The Quiksilver in Memory of Eddie Aikau Big Wave Invitational 1997-98, informational book, received with thanks from George Downing, Contest Director.)

O'ahu

Great Day Trips
and Places to Stay on Oʻahu

Drive 1. The Waiʻanae Coast offers a glimpse of Hawaiʻi beyond the usual tourist routes. Visit Kāneʻākī Heiau (Site 42) and Kāneana Cave (Site 41). Lunch at the golf course at the (closed) Sheraton Hotel near the *heiau*.

Drive 2. A great all day trip that takes in most of the island: Drive east on Kalanianaʻole Highway, stopping to pick up a picnic lunch at Koko Marina Shopping Center, Hawaii Kai. Admire beautiful Hanauma Bay and Hālona Blow Hole (Site 50), visit Ulupō *heiau* (Site 51), and Kualoa Valley (Site 52). Kualoa Regional Park looking out to Chinaman's Hat is a great place to eat a picnic.

      Continue to the great North Shore surfing beaches and Puʻuomahuka Heiau (Site 53).

      Drive back to Honolulu via Kūkaniloko Birthing Stones (Site 43) and the Healing Stones of Wahiawā (Site 44).

Great Places to Stay: Staying at the Turtle Bay Resort on the North Shore is a different experience from busy Waikīkī. The pretty sandy cove is perfect for swimming, and the golf course has beautiful ocean views. Lunch at the poolside bar, watching the big waves roar across the bay, is also memorable. For more information call (808) 293-8811. (Rates: moderate)

      In Waikīkī, the Hilton Hawaiian Village on 10 acres of oceanfront has beautiful gardens and is well situated. Tel.: (808) 949-4321; (800) 445-8667. (Rates: expensive/moderate)

      The New Otani Kaimana Beach Hotel is on the beach opposite the expansive Kapiʻolani Park. Tel.: (808) 923-1555. (Rates: moderate)

Rainbow over Bali Hai cliffs, Princeville, Kaua'i

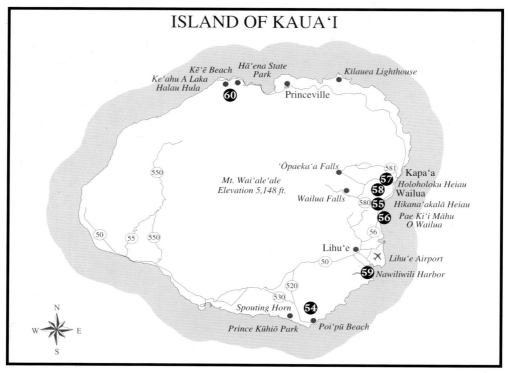

ISLAND OF KAUA'I

54. Prince Kūhiō Park, Po'ipū–
Ancient games people play

> *It is not easy to imagine the scenes presented at one of these great wrestling matches, when not less than four or five thousand persons, dressed in their best apparel and exhibiting every variety of costume and brilliancy or color, were under the influence of excitement. One party was drumming, dancing, and singing in the pride of victory, and the menace of defiance, while the other party was equally vociferous in reciting the achievements of the vanquished, or predicting the shortness of his rival's triumph.*
> *-Reverend William Ellis on Polynesian wrestling (Ellis 1969, 207)*

Hō'AI BAY, with its white sands and sparkling, deep blue water, was an important fishing village, and high chiefs of Kaua'i would often stay here. This peaceful park was an *ali'i* residential site and

Hōʻai Heiau with ancient sports arena

holds remnants of old stone terraces, house sites, irrigation ditches, and a fishing shrine. Small Hōʻai Heiau, consisting of five raised-stone platforms and a large stone-wall enclosure, has an almost perfect chiseled appearance. There is an ancient fishpond where fish were bred for the *aliʻi* and a sports arena where games and sporting competitions were held.

Prince Jonah Kūhiō Kalanianaʻole was born here in 1871. He is revered because of his efforts on behalf of the Hawaiian people. He lived up to his name, Kalanianaʻole, which means literally "the royal chief without measure." He represented Hawaiʻi in the U. S. House of Representatives for more than twenty years and was father of the Hawaiian Homes Commission Act.

The ancient Hawaiian people practiced a great variety of games. They were played mostly in October, at the start of the makahiki, the four-month harvest season when work and war were kapu.

ʻUme, an adulterous sport played by the commoners, was a popular pastime. Players made a bonfire and gathered around it. A man chanted a ribald song and waved a wand of bird feathers, selecting men and women at random. Those selected went out and enjoyed themselves together.

Kilu was a similar game favored by the ali'i. Players sat in a circle. If anyone made a disturbance, they set fire to his clothes. Silence being assured, the kilu, a coconut shell, was placed in front of those who were to play the game. The tally keeper whispered the purpose of the kilu, saying, for instance, "this kilu is a love token; it is a kissing kilu." The tally keeper then gave the kilu to two players. It was thrown at target posts positioned in front of the women. If it hit the target post, the successful player claimed a kiss. They continued to play until a player scored ten, becoming the winner. The reward was the same as in 'ume, but often land or possessions were forfeited instead.

No'a was a betting sport. The players had to guess where the no'a stone was hidden under a kapa cloth. The game made beggars of large numbers of people. Sometimes desperate players staked wives and children. Even the player's own body was sometimes bet. Losing then meant that the player became a slave or moe-pu'u-put to death.

Other milder games included foot racing, throwing the javelin, canoe racing, surf riding, hōlua sledding downhill, juggling, cockfighting, hula, boxing, wrestling, kōnane (checkers), hei (cat's cradle), kimo (jack stones), disc rolling, and kite flying.
(Reference: Malo 1996, 214-34.)

Directions: Take Highway 520, Po'ipū Road, toward Po'ipū. The road forks at the 4-mile mark, just before you reach the beach. Go right on Lāwa'i Road in the direction of the Spouting Horn. A short distance along, you will see Prince Kūhiō Park on your right, opposite a small beach. Drive a couple of miles farther and visit the nearby Spouting Horn Blowhole and hear Hea, the giant dragon lizard, roar in primeval fury.

The Spouting Horn Blowhole, roar of a might dragon lizard

Rising of the sun at Hikina'akalā Heiau

55. Hikina'akalā Heiau, Wailua- *House of the rising sun*

There is casting off!
I am casting thee off!
Do not come to possess my spirit again.
Let me not be a seat for thee again.
Let me not know thee again.
Go and seek some other medium for thyself in another home.
Let it not be me, not at all!
I am wearied of thee!
I am terrified of thee!
I am expelling thee!
Go even to River In Darkness unto Ta'aroa, thy father, Ta'aroa,
the father of all the gods.
Return not again to me.
Behold my family, stricken with sickness.
Thou art taking them.
Thou art a terrible man-devouring god!
-Polynesian chant (Luomala 1986, 65)

FOR CENTURIES, as the rays of the rising sun streaked across the sands, dawn was celebrated with prayers and chants at

Hikina'akalā (Rising of the Sun) Heiau. While reflections of pink clouds floated in the water, *kāhuna* chanted prayers and performed rituals.

The *heiau* was built around A.D. 800 at the mouth of the Wailua River, the first spot in the *kapu* Wailua area touched by the sun's rays. Next to the *heiau* is Hauola (Dew of Life) Place of Refuge. Warriors defeated in war and their families, as well as *kapu* breakers, could flee to this place where they would be safe. The gates were always open, but no pursuer could enter after his prey. The refugee would give offerings, remain a number of days, and then leave a free man. No enemy dared touch him, as this would be a direct affront to the gods. It is reported that on the nights of Kāne, when the moon is a sliver and the night is darkest, the sound of drums and nose flutes played by night marchers can be heard at Hauola.

There was a healing place in the ocean at this site. The sick would dive into the water five times to be cured of their sickness.

Large boulders along the shore have petroglyphs on them, sometimes covered by sand. Tradition says that a sculptor carved idols here and that some of the rocks have the marks of his sculpting. Tools and fishhooks were made here, and ancient shell fishhook chips wash out from the site after heavy rains.

The King's Highway began in the deep ocean and crossed the sand, winding its way up the valley and steep cliffs of Mount Wai'ale'ale to the altar that is still at the misty summit of the mountain.

The Wailua *ali'i* were fine-looking, strong men who were fond of surf riding, which is one of the reasons the highway extended through the breakers. When a king returned from visiting another island, his canoe would approach the shore before those of his warriors, catch the big surf, and ride up the highway to the beach. The king would then be lifted bodily in his canoe and carried up the valley to his house and *heiau*.

Former activities director Lady Ipo of the nearby Holiday Inn Sunspree Resort told us that people still hold ceremonies at the heiau, and their chants are heard at dawn. She said that she was a Christian and didn't pay any attention to these goings-on.

San, whose warm smile greeted us at the resort, had some great stories of ghosts and night marchers. He told us that the security guards at the resort would get together to "talk story," and he loved listening to them.

In one instance, a guard heard loud noises coming from the nearby playground at two o'clock in the morning. He went out to silence the partygoers and saw a procession of men carrying torches walking from the playground to the heiau. The odd thing was that he could only see them from their waists up.

Workmen repairing the resorts on the coast after the destruction of Hurricane Iniki complained about pressing ghosts-heavy weights lying on their chests.

San's favorite story was of the guard who had inspected, closed, and locked the pool restroom and then heard the sounds of running water from a previously dry faucet. He reached in and turned off the faucet. He told his companion about the "boogieman." His companion joked, "Don't take him home with you." That night, as the guard drove home, the battery-operated children's toys in the rear of his vehicle began to jump around on the seat. He had his family blessed by a kahuna.

Directions: Drive on Highway 56 until the turnoff to Lydgate County Beach Park on your right, five miles north of Līhu'e. The remains of the heiau stand in the grounds of the lovely Holiday Inn Sunspree Resort, at the coast, just before the mouth of the Wailua River.

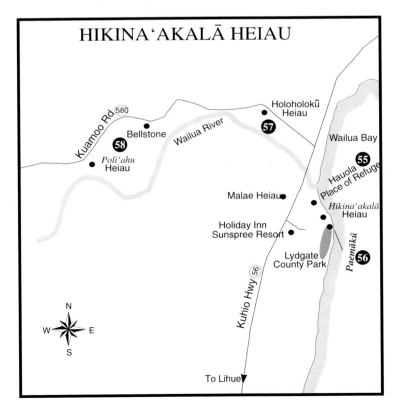

Paemāhū - the rocks/petroglyphs
are often covered by sand and sea

56. Paemāhū o Wailua-
Homosexual dancers

> *The Pōki'i dance of the images,*
> *The images that tilt,*
> *The images with protruding abdomen,*
> *The images with knees spread out and bent,*
> *The images that sway,*
> *Washed by the waves of Wailua,*
> *Is this row of sexless images*
> *They are well known.*
> -"Hula *Ki'i*," Hawaiian chant
> (Barrere, Pukui, and Kelly 1980, 81)

WOODEN IMAGES in strange dancing poses, knees bent, abdomens protruding, once swayed here in the surf. The hula to the images was performed on the beach, and dancers would mimic the images.

Just offshore, at the mouth of the Wailua River, are eight

large rocks and petroglyphs of the dancing figures. Two legends and a hula chant are associated with these rocks and the petroglyphs.

The rocks were said to be young chiefs who were changed into stones. Kapoʻulakīnau, the goddess of mental health, was looking for husbands for her young maidens. She saw the chiefs surfing, borrowed a surfboard, and paddled out, attempting to get the young men to go ashore and woo her companions. The young men were more interested in each other and refused. The angry goddess sent huge waves to crush them, and their bodies turned to stone.

Directions: Turn right off Route 56, five miles from Līhuʻe, at Lydgate County Beach Park. Walk toward the mouth of the river. When you reach the shore you will see a separated group of large rocks and about a dozen petroglyphs on your left. The petroglyphs are sometimes exposed at low tide. Be careful of high surf.

Across the road from the Holiday Inn Sunspree Resort, a trail through the cane fields leads to the sinister Malae *Heiau*. We asked Buddy Peters, our Hawaiian friend and *kupuna*, if we could take his photograph at this *heiau*, and he said that there was no way he was going near the place.

(See map page 181)

57. Holoholokū Heiau and Birthing Stone, Wailua-*Feared death, favored birth*

The child of a chief born at Holoholokū becomes a high chief.
The child of a commoner born at Holoholokū becomes a chief also.
The child of a high chief born outside of Holoholokū is no chief,
a commoner he!
-Hawaiian chant (Kikuchi 1963)

ONE OF the most important *kapu* sites in the sacred area of the Wailua River Valley is the Holoholokū (Run, Run, Stand Fast) Heiau and Pōhaku Hoʻohānau (Birthing Stone).

A child born at the birthing stone gained incredible *mana* and a chiefly status. The rock foundation next to the birthing stone held a special house to shelter the *aliʻi* mother as she gave birth. The rocks were covered with *kapa*. The mother gave birth squatting on mats of pandanus leaves. An attendant squatted behind her, arms wrapped around her stomach, and pushed rhythmically in the Polynesian style to facilitate the birth. Attendants cared for the *ali'i* mother before she entered the shelter of the overhanging ledge to rest after the birth until she could travel.

The sound of a *pahu* (sharkskin-covered drum) would announce the birth of a royal child. The measure of the drumbeat told people far and near whether the child was a girl or a boy.

The rectangular piece of sandstone below the foundation of the shelter is a *kapu* stone set over the remains of a sacrificed dog. Any commoner who stepped on or over this stone would be put to death.

The umbilical cords of the newborn were placed in the *pōhaku piko*. These cords had to be well hidden; if rats ate the cord, the child would grow up to be a disgrace to his parents and a thief. "*Pau piko ka 'iole*" (navel cord gone to the rats) was an insult no Hawaiian wished to hear.

Small Holoholokū Heiau was a much feared place of human sacrifice with a strangely small entrance that was only large enough for a person to crawl through. Within the walls was the house of the *kāhuna* surrounded by images of the gods, with Kū sternly dominant. The *kāhuna* would commune with the gods from the oracle tower, and from it would hang the body of the sacrificed victim.

This richly endowed valley was the residential and religious seat of many powerful chiefs. One of these handsome chiefs was Mo'ikeha. He came to Wailua from Tahiti, where he had loved a beautiful woman called Lu'ukia, by whom he had a son. A jealous enemy had lied to Lu'ukia, convincing her that Mo'ikeha was making fun of her, and Lu'ukia bound herself in cord from her waist to her thighs so that Mo'ikeha could no longer make love to her.

In Wailua, Mo'ikeha eventually married a daughter of the king of Kaua'i, but he still longed for Lu'ukia and his firstborn son. He sent his youngest Hawaiian son, Kila, to Tahiti to find Lu'ukia and to avenge himself on the lying enemy. Kila was successful in a number of ways. He certainly carried out the revenge; he had his warriors hold his father's enemy down in a canoe and urinate on him for two days until the captive drowned. Kila must have been handsome too, for Lu'ukia came to him in the middle of the night. She undid the cords that bound her and, the story says, they "indulged love's desire." Kila's half-brother returned with him to Wailua, bringing the sacred sharkskin drums that were eventually used in all human sacrifice *heiau* and to accompany the hula.

In the 1830s Deborah Kapule, wife of Kaua'i's last king, altered the walls of Malae and Holoholokū Heiau to make cattle and pig pens. By this action, she broke the *kapu* and questioned the power of the gods. With her assistance, a mission was established in Wailua in 1835.

(References: Joesting 1984, 10, 11; Roelofs 1994.)

We climbed a stairway to a hill above the heiau. There, incongruously perched, is a Japanese cemetery. Old, lichen-covered graves lean at strange angles, and blue lanterns sway in the breeze. Are the ancient spirits and the newcomers at peace in this place?

Directions: Take Route 56 from Līhu'e for 5.1 miles. Go inland on Route 580 (Kuamo'o Road). After 0.2 miles, pull over onto the shoulder.

Holoholokū Heiau and birthing stone are located across the road. The birthing stone and the stairway are to the right of the *heiau*.

(See map page 181)

Holoholokū Heiau was a much-feared place of human sacrifice, with a strangely small crawl-through entrance

Holoholokū Heiau

Bellstones, struck when the chiefs arrived, sounded throughout the valley

58. Wailua Valley— *Sacred and forbidden from the mountains to the sea*

In the rising of the sun at Hikina'akalā
In the purification festivities at Hauola
In the row of sexless images at Wailua
In the observations at the point of Alakukui
In the Wai'opua wind of Wailua
In the expansive waters of Wailua
In the renowned surf of Puna
In the changing candlenut tree blossoms of Puna
In the long mountain trail of Kāne
In the births of royalty within Holoholokū
In the burial within Mahunapu'uone
In the refuge and sacrosanct land of Wailua
Nounou, 'A'ahoaka, Maunakapu
Here indeed is Wailuanuiahō'ano.
-Hawaiian chant by E. Kalani Flores (inscribed at site)

THE CHIEFS' ancient trail, the King's Highway, winds its way from the deep ocean beyond the mouth of the Wailua River, across the beach and through the valley. Among the many *heiau* here are tranquil Hikina'akalā Heiau and feared Holoholokū Heiau. Poli'ahu Heiau, a large sacrificial *heiau* dedicated to the goddess of snow, occupies a commanding position at the top of the ridge. Flames from its altars could be seen from Malae Heiau at the bottom of the valley, and sacrificial services were held in tandem.

An altar still exists at the summit of the rain-ravaged Mount Wai'ale'ale. Chiefs, priests, and warriors came annually to make offerings to Kāne, the powerful god of water, sunlight, and all living creatures. The arrival of chiefs was announced by the striking of bellstones and the beating of drums sounding through the valley. Commoners hearing the warning sounds prostrated themselves on the ground. Death was the punishment for gazing at these mighty chiefs.

'Ōpaeka'a Falls, Wailua Valley

Pilgrims traveled by canoe up the sacred Wailua River then marched in procession through the groves of trees, ferns, and bamboo. They pulled themselves up the steep cliff, resting overnight on the ridge. The climb to the summit was slippery, and they ploughed their way through slimy mud, moss-covered trees, and perpetual rain. Mt. Wai'ale'ale is the wettest place in the world. As they neared the 5,148-foot-high summit they chanted praise to Kāne, who had given them this fertile, beautiful valley and their island homes.

A fine-looking young chief from Wailua, Kaumuali'i, became King of Kaua'i at sixteen. He possessed the highest lineage of any chief in all the islands, but his reign was uneasy. He had a powerful rival. Kamehameha the Great craved Kaua'i and planned constant attacks that were thwarted by weather and plagues of illness. Kaua'i remained a separate kingdom, but Kaumuali'i lived in constant fear and even formed a short alliance with Russia to try to protect his domain. The Russian diplomat George Schaeffer named the Hanalei area Schaefferthal and built three forts on Kaua'i.

After the death of Kamehameha I, his heir Liholiho visited Kaua'i and, under the guise of friendship, invited Kaumuali'i on board his luxury yacht. He then sailed back to O'ahu with the captive King of Kaua'i, and here another surprise was in store for Kaumuali'i-the three-hundred pound, six-foot-tall Ka'ahumanu, widow of Kamehameha I. She immediately married both the handsome Kaumuali'i and his handsome son. Missionaries described Kaumuali'i as being finely featured, well dressed, and dignified in manner.

Spirits of the dead chiefs are said to still gather on the upland plains and march as night marchers in ghostly processions with drums and flutes. Listen, then hide!
(References: Joesting 1984, 4, 5, 95-97; Roelofs 1994.)

"If you call them, they will come."
-Buddy Peters, Kaua'i resident

We stayed at a hotel on the coast where the Wailua Valley reaches the sea. It is a strange thought that all these hotels are built on sacred kapu land.

At about five in the morning, I woke up to find something heavy sitting on my foot. I forgot that I was in a hotel; I was half-asleep. It's the cat, I thought. The cat has spent the night on the bed, and he knows he's not allowed to do that. I don't like to kick the cat, so I moved my foot. Then I heard the noise-Clang! Clang! A sharp ringing noise, like stone hitting stone.

"Did you hear that?" Will muttered, tossing in the bed. "That noise has woken me three times tonight. That double-clanging noise. What does it sound like to you?"

"Sounds like bellstones. It sounds just like the noise the bellstones made when I rang them."

I snuggled back under the covers. A pressing ghost and bellstones ringing. Yes!

We were told to speak to Buddy Peters, an expert on Kaua'i's history and tradition. Buddy was at his canoe-rental business at the mouth of the Wailua River. He is a fine-looking Hawaiian man with a curling ponytail and smiling eyes. He invited us into his cabin to "talk story."

"What could we have heard?" I asked. "Could we have heard the bellstones ringing?"

"If you call them, they will come," he answered, somewhat cryptically.

"Call whom?"

"The spirits. You called them. You're open to them coming. They will come!"

What a thought!

"Do you ever call them?" I asked.

"People do. You fast for two days. Light a *kukui*-nut lamp. Drink some *kukui*-nut oil to cleanse your body. Drink some *'awa*. Maybe smoke a little weed. Then you call them. They will come."

"Do you mean you actually see the spirits? Do they look like mist, or what?"

"Sometimes I like to go out on the river in my canoe. August is good. The night of the full moon. I go around midnight. That's a good hour. And I see them clearly. Like I'm seeing you. I see them like a film set, groups sitting or standing on the banks of the river."

Buddy noticed that I was limping. I'd twisted my ankle on the *heiau*. Actually, it had been fine until the pressing ghost sat on it, but we won't go near that.

He handed me a small bag of reddish Hawaiian salt. "Take this with you and keep a *ti* leaf in your shirt," he said. "It's good to have protection when you leave the house."

We left Kaua'i that night. I was limping at the airport.

"I sprained my ankle at the *heiau*," I explained to the porter.

"Oh that's bad," he replied. "And it still hurts even though you prayed?"

"No, I didn't pray."

"Oh, you should pray. You have to go back and pray and make an offering."

The man mopping the floor shook his head. "You have to be very careful at the *heiau*."

Directions: Take Route 56 from Līhu'e for about 5.1 miles. Turn inland on Route 580 (Kuamo'o Road). This road follows the ancient highway. Drive 0.2 miles to the remains of Holoholokū Heiau; to the right of the *heiau* are the birthing stones. At 1.3 miles farther, turn left sharply on a dirt road and drive to its end. The bellstones are below here. Back on Route 580, about 0.1 mile farther, you will come to Poli'ahu Heiau. Continue a short distance to a parking area on the right for a view of beautiful 'Ōpaeka'a Falls.

To explore further, recross the highway and you can see Kamokila, a small, restored Hawaiian village that has an excellent petroglyph.

See map page 181

Bellstones of Wailua Valley

'Alekoko - Menehune Fishpond

59. 'Alekoko, Menehune Fishpond-
Built by the legendary little forest people

> Go to the mountains where you belong,
> Far, far away up there;
> Far away where the red skies lie,
> Away to the road of separation,
> Far away to the clustering yellow bamboo,
> Torch-fisher of the nato of Motutu,
> Picker of eels,
> Thou are the grandchild of the mountains,
> Thou slave of the Arii!
> -Tahitian mele in disdain of the *menehune* (Luomala 1951, 55)

DID MYTHICAL little forest dwellers build this tranquil pond, or was it built by an aboriginal people of smaller build and lower status than the conquering Polynesian settlers?

On Kaua'i there are signs of ancient connections with the Marquesas, and stone implements, language, and styles of *heiau* differ from those found on the other Hawaiian islands. Perhaps the name *menehune* was given by the Tahitians to the early settlers of Hawai'i. The term *manahune*, a variation of *menehune*, was the name for a commoner and a term of derision in Tahiti. The *menehune* legends suggest the mythical little people were happy workers of great strength who worked only at night, passing rocks for long miles in their prolific building feats. Perhaps, however, they were forced into building these structures by the more powerful Polynesians.

Kaua'i, in ancient times, was said to have a population of over 500,000 *menehune*. In the early nineteenth century, a census on the north coast listed sixty-five people who lived in a remote valley and described their nationality as *menehune*.

Legend attributes the building of this nine-hundred-foot-long fishpond, also called 'Alekoko (Rippling Blood) Pond, to the *menehune*, who built it at the request of a lazy relative called Pi. They agreed to build it on condition that they would not be watched, and they worked so hard that their blood rippled in the water. When they discovered that they were being spied on, they returned to the forest, leaving holes in the wall. Pi chose not to further annoy the *menehune* (a wise move, as they had the reputation for turning annoying people into stone) and paid them with their favorite food, a multitude of red shrimp. Their happy shouts echoed through the valley.

The pond was used by chiefs as a storehouse for *moi* and mullet. The pond was *kapu*, but commoners were allowed to eat some species of fish. Guardian spirits protected the pond. According to Niumalu residents, these guardians were royal children who possessed supernatural powers. The girl could change to a dragon lizard and the boy to a shark.
(Reference: Luomala 1951, 6-68.)

Directions: From Līhu'e and Highway 50, take Nāwiliwili Road to Niumalu Road. Turn right and follow it to Hulemalu Road. Turn right and proceed to a marked lookout, about half a mile uphill, below which is 'Alekoko Pond. The blue pond and massive Hoary Head Mountains make a picturesque scene.

Ke-ahu-a-Laka hula platform with altar to Laka at cliff face

60. Ke-ahu-a-Laka Hālau Hula, Kē'ē Beach, Hā'ena-Altar of Laka, *goddess of dance, temple of hula*

> *Far off as the ridges of the upland.*
> *Behold Laka standing on the mountain,*
> *Wreathed in mist, dwelling with the summit cloud.*
> *Laka, goddess of the hula . . .*
> -forest chant in praise of Laka (Pukui and Korn 1973, 45)

THE MAGIC of the misty, towering *pali*, the lilting music, throbbing drums, and beautiful dancers; this is the land of Laka, goddess of the hula. The scenic, winding road past Hanalei to the Nā Pali coast ends at Kē'ē Beach. A coastal path leads several hundred feet to two ancient temples.

Only fragmented terraces remain of Ka-ulu-Paoa Heiau, named for a famous hula master and situated near the rocky shore of Kēʻē Beach. The *heiau* is said to have been built by the hardworking *menehune.*

Farther uphill, past the broken stone terraces, is the *hālau hula* (house of hula). A flat platform is all that remains of the temple dedicated to the goddess Laka. It is a dizzying experience to dance here with the waves crashing below and the fluted green cliffs soaring above.

The *hālau hula,* where the dancers were trained, was sponsored by the *aliʻi.* The training was strict and had many *kapu.* Dancers could not cut their hair or nails for the period they were in training. Certain foods were *kapu,* and no sexual intercourse was allowed.

The *kumu hula* (teacher of dance) composed chants honoring the *aliʻi* family and acted as *kahuna* of the *heiau.* Chants for a high *aliʻi* would involve prayer chants, genealogy chants, and name chants. The spoken word contained powerful *mana,* and often the sacred names of gods and divine chiefs were uttered. These chants were treated carefully. A mistaken syllable might offend the god or change the meaning and would then cause the dancer's death. "In the word is life, in the word is death." (Elbert and Mahoe 1970, 19). Family chants are still given great respect today.

After the training, a test was given to see if all the rules had been kept. The students swam from the beach to the rocks, passing a shark who lurked in the reef and attacked those who had not been strictly obedient. Impressive celebrations followed graduation, including fire-throwing from the cliffs of nearby 1,600-foot Makana Mountain. The glowing firebrands would glide into the sea, watched by crowds of people and rows of canoes.

The erotic dancing of the islands of Polynesia was also a form of worship. The purpose of these dances was to bring about fertility in nature. The dances were designed to bring into action the *mana* of the gods, who were believed to be aroused by the same emotions as men, and on whose procreative activities the fertility of humans, the earth, and the sea depended. Men danced the fertility dances at the *heiau.* The reproductive powers of the chiefs were celebrated and many a Hawaiian chief had his own *mele maʻi,* or genital chant, with appropriate descriptions. Such a chief was King Kalākaua, whose chant credited him with *hālala,* or being very well endowed.

Waves crash on the rocky coast below the hula platform

Under the influence of the early missionaries, who were horrified by the bare breasts and exposed flesh of the hula dancers, in 1830 Queen Kaʻahumanu forbade the hula. Similarly, in 1835 Kamehameha III banned the hula, following the wishes of his missionary advisors. In 1874 King Kalākaua revived it. He called the hula "the language of the heart and the heartbeat of the Hawaiian people." In hula lies the rich, dramatic history of Hawaiʻi presented in sensual, visual, and audible forms.

There is a legend that a boy and a girl at the hālau hula fell in love despite the *kapu* on such relationships. They fled just before graduation, praying to Laka for forgiveness. The chiefess of the school followed them. She caught the girl hiding in a cave and killed her. The young man ran up the ridge, but she caught him at the top and killed him too. The goddess Laka turned the lovers into flowers-beach naupaka and mountain *naupaka*. Each shrub bears only half a flower, so that like the lovers, they are incomplete when separated. When they are brought together, they make one perfect flower.
(References: Joesting 1984, 32; Kanahele 1986, 94.)

In recent years, this powerful and graceful dance has been revived. Hula dancers still come to this temple platform to dance the hula and offer leis and *ti* leafs. Umbilical cords of newborn babies are still placed in rock crevices so the children may benefit from the strong *mana* here.

Each year hula festivals are held in recognition of the importance of this traditional dance. They include the Merrie Monarch Hula Festival in Hilo in April, the Kamehameha Day Hula and Chant at Brigham Young University Hawai'i at Lā'ie, O'ahu on June 11, the Prince Lot Festival in mid-July at Moanalua Gardens, O'ahu, and the *Makahiki* Celebration at Waimea Falls Park, O'ahu, in October. Other *hālau hula* groups, such as Island Breeze and Spirit of Joy, also use hula expression to give glory to God.

Directions: Kē'ē Beach is at the end of Highway 56, forty miles north of Līhu'e. To the left of the beach follow a coastal path several hundred feet along the cove until it turns uphill to the *heiau*. Kē'ē Lagoon has huge shady trees, swimming, and great snorkeling. The start of the incredibly scenic Nā Pali trail is across from the parking area. Nearby Limahuli Garden is a "living classroom" where you can wander along trails and learn about Hawaiian plants in a setting of spectacular beauty.

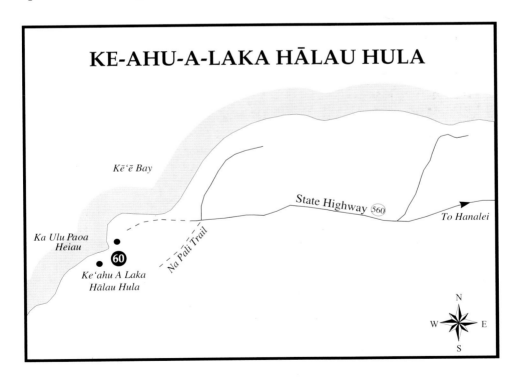

Great Day Trips
and Places to Stay on Kaua'i

Drive 1. Visit Wailua Valley for a morning of exploring. Explore Hikina'akalā Heiau (Site 55) to swim with fish in the lava pools, Paemāhū o Wailua (Site 56), Holoholokū Heiau and Birthing Stone (Site 57), Wailua Valley and Poli'ahu Heiau (Site 58), 'Ōpaeka'a Falls and Kamokila Hawaiian Village.

It's fun to rent a canoe (call Wailua Kayak and Canoe at 821-1188) and paddle up the river to the Fern Grotto.

Great Place to Stay: The lovely, spacious Holiday Inn Sunspree Resort takes pride in its sweeping ocean views, ancient *heiau*, and city of refuge. It also has the only safe swimming on this stretch of coast-beautiful lava pools full of rainbow-colored fish. The adjacent playground was designed by children of Kaua'i. For more information call (888) 823-5111 or (808) 823-6000. (Rates: moderate)

Drive 2. A perfect drive follows the scenic coast to Ke-ahu-a-Laka Hālau Hula (Site 60). At the end of the road, explore lush Limahuli Garden, and swim at perfect Kē'ē Beach.

Back in picturesque Hanalei, admire the Bali Hai Cliffs, visit the beautiful old church and mission house, and spend the evening socializing at Tahiti Nui.

Great Places to Stay: The Princeville Resort offers sumptuous accommodation with incomparable views over the magic Bali Hai cliffs of Hanalei. Breakfast on the terrace is a blissful experience; For more information call (800) 826-4400 or (808) 826-9644. (Rates: expensive)

The Cliffs at Princeville offers one-bedroom condo units that are great for families. Ask for directions down the cliff to the ocean rock pool. It may still have a resident sea turtle. For further information call (800) 367-8024 or (808) 826-6219. (Rates: moderate)

EPILOGUE

Whatever you desire, believe you have it, and you shall have it.
The wise kāhuna believed in the power of the mind and in the power of
words. If you would like to test for yourself a part of this word power,
select a goal or something material that you would like to have. Choose
something that is beyond your means, but not too much so. Write the
name of the desired goal or object on a card, and put it where you can see
it frequently. Every time you see the card, visualize your goal or the
object, and think how much you want it.

    Of all the magical constituents in accomplishing a purpose
through the power of words, intense desire was considered the most
important. Do this every day until your desire becomes a reality. And
may the mana be with you!
(Reference: Beckley 1987, 42.)

Bibliography

Abbott, Isabella. *Lā'au Hawai'i: Traditional Hawaiian Uses of Plants.* Honolulu: Bishop Museum Press, 1992.

Adler, Jacob, and Robert M. Kamins. *The Fantastic Life of Walter Murray Gibson: Hawai'i's Minister of Everything.* Honolulu: University of Hawai'i Press, 1986.

Answar, Yasmin. "Healers Worry about Legacy." *Honolulu Advertiser,* 8 November 1998.

Bailey, Paul Dayton. *Those Kings and Queens of Old Hawai'i: A Mele to Their Memory.* Tucson, Ariz.: Westernlore Press, 1988.

Barrere, Dorothy B., Mary Kawena Pukui, and Marion Kelly. *Hula: Historical Perspectives.* Pacific Anthropological Records 30. Honolulu: Bernice P. Bishop Museum, 1980.

Beckley, Timothy Green. *Kāhuna Power: Authentic Chants and Prayers.* New Brunswick, N.J.: Inner Light, 1987.

Beckwith, Martha Warren. *Hawaiian Mythology.* 1940. Honolulu: University of Hawai'i Press, 1970.

———. *The Kumulipo: A Hawaiian Creation Chant.* 1951. Honolulu: University of Hawai'i Press, 1972.

Bisignani, J. D. *Hawaii Handbook.* Chico, Calif.: Moon Publications, 1994.

Carlson, Doug. *Punchbowl: The National Memorial Cemetery of the Pacific.* Honolulu: Island Heritage, 1992.

Chiles, William "Pila." *The Secrets and Mysteries of Hawai'i.* Deerfield Beach, Fla.: Health Communications, 1992.

Ching, Linda, and Robin Stephens. *Powerstones: Letters to a Goddess.* Honolulu: Hawaiian Goddess Publishing Company, 1994.

Clark, John R. K. *Beaches of the Big Island.* Honolulu: University of Hawai'i Press, 1985.

Cox, J. Halley, with Edward Stasack. *Hawaiian Petroglyphs.* Honolulu: Bishop Museum Press, 1970.

Creamer, Beverley. "A Healing Touch." *Honolulu Advertiser,* 21 September 1988.

Daws, Gavan. *Shoal of Time: A History of the Hawaiian Islands.* New York: Macmillan, 1968.

Doughty, Andrew, and Harriet Friedman. *Hawai'i: The Big Island Revealed.* Lihu'e, Kaua'i: Wizard Publications, 1997.

Dudley, Michael. *A Hawaiian Nation I: Man, Gods and Nature.* Honolulu: Nā Kāne o Ka Malo Press, 1990.

Elbert, Samuel H., and Noelani Mahoe. *Nā Mele o Hawai'i Nei: 101 Hawaiian Songs.* Honolulu: University of Hawai'i Press, 1970.

Ellis, William. *Polynesian Researches.* 1842. Rutland, Vt.: Charles E. Tuttle, 1969.

Emerson, Nathaniel B. *Pele and Hi'iaka: A Myth from Hawai'i.* 1915. Rutland, Vt.: Charles E. Tuttle, 1978.

Emory, Kenneth Pike. *The Island of Lāna'i: A Survey of Native Culture.*
1924. Honolulu: Bishop Museum Press, 1969.

Emory, Kenneth Pike, Patrick Carlton McCoy, and Dorothy B. Barrere.
*Archaeological Survey: Kahalu'u and Keauhou, North Kona,
Hawai'i.* Department of Anthropology Report 71-4. Honolulu:
Bernice P. Bishop Museum, 1971.

Fornander, Abraham. *Collection of Hawaiian Antiquities and Folk-Lore.*
Vols. 4 and 5. Honolulu: Bernice P. Bishop Museum, 1917–20.

————. *Selections from Fornander Hawaiian Antiquities and Folk-Lore.*
Ed. Samuel H. Elbert. Honolulu: University of Hawai'i Press,
1959.

Gallagher, Charles F. *Hawai'i and Its Gods.* New York: Weatherhill, 1975.

Gay, Lawrence Kainoahou. *True Stories of Lāna'i.* Honolulu: Mission
Press, 1965.

Grant, Glen. *Obake Files: Ghostly Encounters in Supernatural Hawai'i.*
Honolulu: Mutual Publishing, 1996.

Gutmanis, June. *Kahuna Lā'au Lapa'au.* Honolulu: Island Heritage,
1977.

————. *Na Pule Kahiko: Ancient Hawaiian Prayers.* Honolulu: Editions
Limited, 1983.

————. *Pōhaku, Hawaiian Stones.* Lā'ie, Hawai'i: Brigham Young
University, 1986.

Handy, E. S. Craighill, et al. *Ancient Hawaiian Civilization: A Series of
Lectures Delivered at Kamehameha Schools.* Rutland, Vt.:
Charles E. Tuttle, 1965.

Handy, E. S. Craighill, and E. G. Handy. *Native Planters in Old Hawai'i:
Their Life, Lore, and Environment.* 1972. Honolulu: Bishop
Museum Press, 1991.

Heselton, Philip. *Leylines.* London: Hodder and Stoughton, 1999.

Hogue, Charles. "Pūowaina, Consecrated Hill." *Paradise of the Pacific,*
October 1949, 30.

James, Van. *Ancient Sites of Hawai'i: Archaeological Places of Interest
on the Big Island of Hawai'i.* Honolulu: Mutual Publishing, 1996.

Joesting, Edward. *Hawai'i, an Uncommon History.* New York: W.
W. Norton & Co., 1972.

————. *Kaua'i: The Separate Kingdom.* Honolulu: University of
Hawai'i Press, 1984.

Johnson, Rubellite Kawena. *Kumulipo: The Hawaiian Hymn of
Creation.* Honolulu: Topgallant Publishing, 1981.

Kalākaua, David. *The Legends and Myths of Hawai'i: The Fables and
Folklore of a Strange People.* Honolulu: Mutual Publishing, 1990.

Kamakau, Samuel Mānaikalani. *Ka Po'e Kahiko: The People of Old.*

Honolulu: Bishop Museum Press, 1964.

———. *Tales and Traditions of the People of Old: Nā Moʻolelo a ka Poʻe Kahiko*. Honolulu: Bishop Museum Press, 1991.

———. *Ruling Chiefs of Hawaiʻi*. 1961. Honolulu: Kamehameha Schools Press, 1992.

Kanahele, George Heʻeu Sanford. *Kū Kanaka Stand Tall: A Search for Hawaiian Values*. Honolulu: University of Hawaiʻi Press, 1986.

Kikawa, Daniel. *Perpetuated in Righteousness*. Kāneʻohe, Hawaiʻi: Aloha Ke Akua Publishing, 1994.

Kikuchi, William. *Archaeological Survey and Excavations on the Island of Kauaʻi*. Committee for the Preservation of Hawaiian Culture and Committee for the Preservation and Study of Hawaiian Language, Art, and Culture. Honolulu: University of Hawaiʻi at Mānoa, 1963.

Kirch, Patrick Vinton. *Feathered Gods and Fishhooks: An Introduction to Hawaiian Archaeology and Prehistory*. Honolulu: University of Hawaiʻi Press, 1985.

———. *Legacy of the Landscape*. Honolulu: University of Hawaiʻi Press, 1996.

Kuykendall, Ralph S. *The Hawaiian Kingdom*. Vol. 1. Honolulu: University of Hawaiʻi Press, 1938.

Luomala, Katharine. *The Menehune of Polynesia and Other Mythical Little People of Oceania*. Bulletin 203. Honolulu: Bernice P. Bishop Museum, 1951.

———. *Voices on the Wind: Polynesian Myths and Chants*. Honolulu: Bishop Museum Press, 1986.

Malo, David. *Hawaiian Antiquities*. 1951. Honolulu: Bishop Musuem Press, 1996.

McAllister, J. Gilbert. *Archaeology of Oʻahu*. 1933. Millwood, N.Y.: Krauss, 1985.

McBride, L. R. *Petroglyphs of Hawaiʻi*. Hilo: Petroglyph Press, 1969.

Morrill, S. *The Kahunas, the Black and White Magicians of Hawaiʻi*, Boston, Brandon Press Publishers, 1969

Pearson, Richard J. "The Archaeology of Hāna: Preliminary Survey of Waiʻānapanapa State Park." *Hawaiʻi State Archaeological Journal* 70, no. 2 (1970).

Piercy, La Rue W. *Hawaiʻi's Missionary Saga: Sacrifice and Godliness in Paradise*. Honolulu: Mutual Publishing, 1992.

Pukui, Mary K., and Samuel H. Elbert. *Hawaiian Dictionary*. Honolulu: University of Hawaiʻi Press, 1986.

Pukui, Mary K., Samuel H. Elbert, and Esther T. Mookini. *Place Names of Hawaii*. Honolulu: University of Hawaiʻi Press, 1989.

Pukui, Mary K., E. W. Haertig, and Catharine A. Lee. *Nānā I Ke Kumu (Look to the Source)*. 2 vols. Honolulu: Hui Hānai, 1972.

Pukui, Mary K., and Alfons L. Korn. *The Echo of Our Song: Chants and Poems of the Hawaiians*. Honolulu: University of Hawai'i Press, 1973.

Ramirez, Tino. "Birthing Stones Open for Tours." *Honolulu Advertiser*, 1 June 1998.

Richards, William. *Memoir of Keōpūolani*. Boston: Crocker and Brewster, 1825.

Roelofs, Faith. *In the Land of Nā Wai 'Eha: Waihee Trail and Haleki'i*. Honolulu: Moanalua Gardens Foundation, 1993.

———. *Footsteps of the Ali'i: Wailua Basin and Heiau Complex*. Honolulu: Moanalua Gardens Foundation, 1994.

Sahlins, Marshall David. *Historical Metaphors and Mythical Realities: Structure in the Early History of the Sandwich Islands Kingdom*. Association for Social Anthropology in Oceania Special Publication 1. Ann Arbor: University of Michigan Press, 1981.

Schmitt, Robert C. *Historical Statistics of Hawaii*. Honolulu: University of Hawai'i Press, 1977.

Spalding, Philip, III. *Moloka'i*. Honolulu: Westwind Press, 1984.

Steiger, Brad. *Kahuna Magic*. West Chester, Pa.: Schiffer Publishing, 1971.

Sterling, E. *Sites of Maui*. Honolulu: Bishop Museum Press, 1998.

Sterling, Elspeth, and Catherine Summers. *Sites of O'ahu*. Honolulu: Bishop Museum Press, 1978.

Stokes, John F. G. *Heiau of the Island of Hawai'i: A Historic Survey of Native Hawaiian Temples*. Honolulu: Bishop Museum Press, 1991.

Summers, Catherine. *Moloka'i: A Site Survey*. Honolulu: Bishop Museum Press, 1971.

Thom, Wah Chan. *The Story of Mānoa Chinese Cemetery: With a Discussion of Ancestor Worship*. Honolulu: Lin Yee Chung Association, 1985.

Westervelt, William. "The Sacrificial Rock of Punchbowl." *Honolulu Star-Bulletin*, 25 October 1919.

Glossary of Hawaiian Terms

akua. God, goddess.

ali'i. Chief or person of high rank.

'anā 'anā. Evil sorcery.

'aumakua. Family or personal god; pl. *'aumākua.*

'awa. A narcotic drink.

hālau. A house used for hula instruction.

heiau. A place of worship or where sacrifices were offered.

hōlua. A sled used on grassy slopes or stone slides.

hula. The dance of ancient Hawai'i.

'ili'ili. Small waterworn pebbles used to pave house floors.

imu. Underground oven.

kāhili. Standard ornamented with feathers.

kahuna. Priest, sorcerer, or expert; pl. *kāhuna.*

kalo. The taro plant.

Kāne. The creator god, a major deity of ancient Hawai'i.

kapa. Tapa or bark cloth.

kapu. Taboo, sacred, or forbidden.

ki. The ti plant.

Kū. The god of war, a major deity of ancient Hawai'i.

kukui. Candlenut tree, the nuts were dried and burned for light.

kū'ula. A stone image of the god of fishermen.

lele kawa. To leap into water feet first.

Lua. Hand-to-hand fighting, bone breaking, noosing, leaping, and twisting spears.

Luakini. A temple in which rites were dedicated to the war-god, Kū; a temple of human sacrifice.

lei. A garland or necklace of flowers or feathers.

lele. A stand constructed of wooden timbers on which offerings were placed.

mauka. Inland, toward the mountains.

maka'āinana. Commoner.

mākāhā. The sluice gate of a fishpond.

*makai.*Toward the sea.

mana. Supernatural or divine power.

menehune. A legendary race of small people who worked at night.

noni. The Indian mulberry.

pali. Cliff or precipice.

piko. Navel, umbilical cord.

pōhaku. Stone.

pu'uhonua. A place of refuge.

wahine. Woman.

Index

About the Authors

Ellie and William Crowe have explored every continent and lived in Australia, South Africa, and the U.S.A. Islands are their favorite places, and for the last twelve years they have traveled the Hawaiian Islands and read extensively about Hawai'i's history and legends. They are members of the Hawaiian Historical Society.

Ellie is an author whose books include Little Princess Ka'iulani, The Littlest Paniolo, and The Lonely Boy Who Became a Mighty King, a biography of the childhood of King Kamehameha I-all published by Island Heritage.

A commercial real estate broker and photographer, William holds liberal arts and law degrees from University of Sydney, Australia. Their work is featured in the Travel Channel's "Places of Mystery" series and "Haunted Hawai'i" on the History Channel. The authors have three children and live in Honolulu, Hawai'i.

NOTE

NOTE